MW01230670

Corporate
Tragedies

Corporate Tragedies

PRODUCT TAMPERING, SABOTAGE, AND OTHER CATASTROPHES

by
Ian I. Mitroff
and Ralph H. Kilmann

PRAEGER

PRAEGER SPECIAL STUDIES • PRAEGER SCIENTIFIC

Library of Congress Cataloging in Publication Data

Mitroff, Ian I.
    Corporate tragedies.

    Includes index.
    1. Organizational effectiveness. I. Kilmann, Ralph H.
II. Title.
HD58.9.M57   1984   658.4   84-6764
ISBN 0-03-064104-7 (alk. paper)

The following trademarks are used throughout the book: Tylenol, owned by MacNeil Consumer Products Company; Rely, owned by Procter and Gamble Company; Tampax, owned by Tampax Inc.; Custer's Revenge, Bachelor Party, and Beat 'Em & Eat 'Em, owned by American Multiple Industries; Cracker Jack, owned by Cracker Jack; Ball Park, owned by Hygrade Food Products Corporation; Rubik's Cube, owned by Ideal Toy Corporation; Kilmann-Saxton Culture-Gap Survey, owned by Organizational Design Consultants Inc.; Activision, owned by Activision Inc.

Published in 1984 by Praeger Publishers
CBS Educational and Professional Publishing,
a Division of CBS Inc.
521 Fifth Avenue, New York, NY 10175 USA

©1984 by Ian I. Mitroff
and Ralph H. Kilmann

All rights reserved

456789   052   9876545321

Printed in the United States of America
on acid-free paper

The only thing necessary for the triumph of evil is for good men to do nothing.

—Edmund Burke

Humankind cannot bear very much reality.

—T. S. Eliot

Contents

Preface

The placing of cyanide in Tylenol did more than disgust and horrify us—it filled us with anger and sadness as well. It was a clear signal: the ways in which most of us have been trained to think are no longer adequate to cope with a world grown increasingly complex, unpredictable, and evil.

Day by day with increasing frequency are accounts in newspapers and magazines, on the radio and TV of actions that boggle the mind. What was once unimaginable and unthinkable seems to happen to executives and organizations on an almost daily basis. Products and services that were produced and provided under the best intentions of doing good become sabotaged and converted into agents of evil. The products, services, and industries, and most basic of all, our beliefs in them, that once guaranteed our economic success now seem to be the very things from which we need protection. We have indeed met the enemy and he is not only the evil threat from without but he is also the evil from within that resides in all of us.

This book is how to think about and cope with the kinds of tragedies that are happening to organizations of all kinds. In a world facing the biggest tragedy and unthinkable of all, nuclear holocaust, the reader has good reason to ask why we have deliberately restricted our focus to tragedies committed against organizations. Our answer is that society is built up of organizations. Governments, industry, education and health care, are all made-up of organizations that exist in an environment of other organizations. Most of our waking lives are spent employed in such organizations and acting as members of these organizations. Only a small proportion of our time is spent as individuals qua individuals. All of the tragedies and unthinkable acts that affect organizations or are created by organizations must ultimately be managed by them.

Because organizations are our focus, we thought of titling this book, "When Bad Things Happen to Good Organizations." We fortunately chose not to do this for obvious reasons. Still it captures part of the essence of this text. Most of the tragedies that have occurred have happened to organizations which are themselves blameless. This makes them even more tragic.

Another title we considered using was "What They Didn't Teach You, What They Couldn't Teach You in Business School, But What You Need to Know in Order to Survive Future Shock." We rejected this title because of its length. Still, it captures pretty well the spirit of the book.

Finally, a word of caution to the reader. It is a strong testimony to the fact that most people prefer to avoid thinking about the unpleasant thus many may find the events described in this book "depressing." We understand this reaction only too well for we have encountered it on numerous occasions, whenever we have spoken to audiences about the material contained in this book. We would caution the reader however to do his/her best not to give in to this emotion however understandable it is.

As professional social scientists we have been trained, much like medical doctors, to analyze social illnesses whether we happen to like them or not. As a result, we realize that an essential part in coping with tragic events is to develop a certain emotional strength, but not callousness, toward it. Most managers or executives have not been prepared either intellectually or emotionally to face tragic events. This is a shame, if not a disaster, in today's world. For the fact is, like it or not, unthinkable and tragic acts against corporations exist and occur with greater frequency than ever before. Management has no choice but to face up to them. One of our most essential points is that thinking about the unthinkable is fundamentally part and parcel of thinking strategically about the totality of an organization. To avoid thinking about the unthinkable is to avoid facing up to an organization's potential. It is to be unable to meet its essential problems as well as to grasp its opportunities.

Even though all tragedies can not be prevented from occurring, one can nonetheless think about nearly every aspect that is connected with them. In short, if the reader is willing to face the unthinkable squarely in the eye, then one can do more to cope with it than one might have thought initially.

We owe so much to so many in teaching us to think that we could never mention them all by name. At the head of the list, however, would be our mentors: Russell L. Ackoff, C. West Churchman, Thomas A. Cowan, Kenneth D. Mackenzie, and Robert Tannenbaum. They have provided us with a lifetime of inspiration. They have encouraged us in every way they could to view the world as a very rich environment in which one could learn many things if one was only willing to give up some traditional academic prejudices. In this regard, some of our best teachers have been practitioners. We thought we were the ones teaching them. How wrong we were. The biggest unthinkable for a university professor to admit is that he might be taught something valuable from those on the "outside." According to this criterion, Vincent P. Barabba, Peter F. Mathias, and Roy Serpa have been among our very best teachers.

No book would be complete without mentioning some of our closest colleagues: Warren Bennis, William Dunn, Craig Lundberg, Richard O. Mason, Thomas L. Saaty, and Gerald Zaltman. We owe much to every one of them.

Last, there are our families, which in a world that seems increasingly mad, provide what's sadly becoming the rarest quality of all—love. They're distinctive characters in every best sense of the term.

Corporate
Tragedies

1

Introduction:
What Kind of World Is It
Where Even Pickles Aren't Safe
Anymore?

I returned, and saw under the sun, that the race is not to the swift, nor
the battle to the strong, neither yet bread to the wise, nor yet riches to
men of understanding, nor yet favour to men of skill; but time and chance
happeneth to them all. For man also knoweth not his time: as the fishes
that are taken in an evil net, and as the birds that are caught in the snare;
so are the sons of men snared in an evil time, when it falleth suddenly
upon them.

Ecclesiastes 9:11–12

This book is about the growing number and increasing frequency of
the unspeakable and unbelievable things that are happening to organizations of all kinds. Its purpose is to help all those connected with organizations to face up to them, to think about them, and to cope with them
more effectively. Even though no one can prevent all tragedies from occurring, it is possible nonetheless to think about nearly every aspect connected with them.

The increase and frequency of tragic acts committed against organizations forces us to acknowledge that evil is an ever present reality in today's business world. Evil is one of the most potent forces shaping today's organizations.

In this chapter five basic kinds of tragedies will be presented. We
make no claim that these five exhaust all such kinds, but they are sufficient to get any organization thinking about the worst that could happen
to it. Any organization that does not take seriously every one of these
cases is living in a dream world.

1

TAMPERING, THE EVIL FROM WITHOUT:
THE CASE OF TYLENOL

Perhaps no other case in recent memory brings home as strongly the impact of a major tragedy on a corporation than the events associated with Tylenol. A November 1982 article in the popular business magazine *Fortune* reveals an eerie side to the whole case.[1] An ominous premonition was in the air before the heinous acts soon to be associated with Tylenol had occurred. Early in September 1982 at the annual three-day strategic planning retreat of Johnson and Johnson, the parent company of McNeil, J & J's Chairman James Burke mused at how lucky they were to be in an industry that had such extremely profitable brands. However, he reflected out loud, "What if something happened to one of [their main products], like Tylenol?" "Nothing," he noted, "is impregnable." Not only could nobody come up with anything that could dampen what seemed to be an extraordinarily successful business but Burke "took some kidding. . .for worrying about things [he didn't] have to."[2]

Then the unthinkable occurred.[3]

On September 29, 1982, two brothers, Adam and Steven Janus, and Mary Kellerman, of two different suburbs outside of Chicago, died from taking Extra-Strength Tylenol capsules. Cyanide, a deadly poison, had been injected into the capsules. One day later, Mary Reiner and Mary McFarland, again of Chicago suburbs, also died of cyanide poisoning. Tylenol was identified as the culprit in all the cases. More specifically, the poisonous capsules were traced to manufacturer's lot number MC 2880. Even worse, later deaths were to be traced to additional lots 1910 MD and MC 2738. The worst had happened. Not only was Tylenol poisoned but the disaster had widened to multiple lots. Nobody knew how many different lots were infected.

J & J reacted promptly. All 93,400 bottles of lot number MC 2880 were immediately recalled. A day later all 171,000 bottles of lot number 1910 MD were also recalled.

On October 4, 1982, the FDA (Federal Drug Administration) ordered its 19 laboratories to begin the testing of Extra-Strength Tylenol capsules. The tested capsules were drawn from a nationwide random sample from store shelves.

That same day, the widow of Adam Janus filed a $15 million damage suit against J & J. Two other suits were to be filed later asking for damages around $35 million. Most severe of all, a fourth suit was to be filed demanding that refunds be granted to everyone in the country who bought Tylenol that year![4] Estimates of the potential costs of that suit ran as high as $600 million.

On October 5, the next day, the poisoning had spread across the nation. Three bottles of Extra-Strength Tylenol laced with strychnine were found in Oroville, California.

On October 6, J & J sent telex messages to approximately 15,000 nationwide retailers and distributors. The messages asked them to remove all 11 million bottles of regular and Extra-Strength Tylenol from their shelves.

The initial cost to J & J was measured in more than dollars alone.[5] The tragedy took its toll in psychological impact as much as it did in dollars. It affected the confidence and the security that J & J's executives had in their own products as much as it did the public's. The best analogy is that for the executives of J & J and McNeil it was like going through a death in the family. The very essence, the very cornerstone, of the analgesic business was built on one key word: trust. People took Tylenol because it was recommended to them by their physicians or because it was given to them in hospitals. They took it because, in Burke's words, "they were not well and [they were] in a highly emotional state."[6] The questions now, as the writer of the *Fortune* article, Thomas Moore, put it, were: if emotions were responsible for the initial taking of Tylenol and the subsequent brand identification with it, would those same emotions turn against Tylenol because people wouldn't want to take a chance with a product whose name was now emotionally charged in a negative sense? If the name Tylenol was initially associated with the very epitome of goodness and trust, would it now be associated with the very epitome of distrust and evil? Who could blame a public for not willing to risk its trust?[7]

Even if dollars alone were not sufficient to measure the full impact of such a tragedy, the dollars are impressive nonetheless. They were anything but negligible or trivial. In 1975, McNeil began promoting Tylenol aggressively as an alternate pain reliever for those who suffered from upset stomachs and other side effects of aspirin. By 1982, Tylenol had an incredible 35 percent of the $1 billion analgesic market. As a measure of Tylenol's significance to J & J, it accounted for an estimated 7 percent of J & J's worldwide sales and anywhere from an estimated 15 percent to 20 percent of its total profits in 1981. Before the poisonings, McNeil's executives confidently predicted that Tylenol would capture 50 percent of the market, if not more, by 1986.

All in all, J & J recalled some 31 million bottles with a retail value of over $100 million. As a result, its third-quarter earnings dropped from 78 cents a share in 1981 to 51 cents in 1982. Security analysts projected a 70 percent drop in normal $100 million in 1982 fourth-quarter over-the-counter sales of Tylenol products. In 1983, Tylenol had been predicted to earn a half-billion dollars in sales. After the tragedy, analysts predicted that J & J would be fortunate if it earned half of that.[8]

The Tylenol tragedy is our first and perhaps most prominent example of the kind of unthinkable, tragic act that can happen to any kind of organization. A central, mainstay product (or service) from which the organization derives a significant amount of its income and for which the public has considerable brand recognition and loyalty is designed under the original intention of doing good. The properties of the product (service) are then altered, drastically so, by the injection of foreign substances into it. The product (service) is then converted into an agent for doing evil to its unsuspecting consumers. As a result, both the consumers and the producers of the product (service) suffer considerable loss. Every organization is now vulnerable to this kind of loss, tragedy, and threat.

When we say that this kind of thing is unthinkable, we mean it in at least two distinct senses. One, it is unbelievable—totally unthinkable—that anyone would actually do such a terrible thing to other human beings. Most of us find it difficult to imagine what kind of mind could actually do such things. It is not beyond the imagination of most of us to think violent acts. Indeed we do this all the time without conscious awareness. It is however beyond normalcy for our violent impulses to cross over the barrier, however fragile it is, from mere fantasizing to their actual enactment in reality.[9]

Two, other than preventive packaging, it is hard if not seemingly impossible to know what one could have done beforehand to prevent such tragedies. In a nation of approximately 226,500,000 people,[10] it seems clearly impossible to predict which specific individuals would do such a thing let alone to pinpoint their exact location and time of striking.

On both counts we feel absolutely stymied. We feel helpless, at the mercy of an uncontrollable, unpredictable environment. As one writer put it, commenting on what the Tylenol tragedy meant to him: "One man in California threatened to poison jars of pickles in Safeway stores unless paid a large sum.

"Actually, it seems a little astonishing to me, living in a world where not even pickle jars are safe...."[11]

UNPLANNED, UNWANTED DEFECTS,
THE EVIL FROM WITHIN:
THE CASE OF RELY TAMPONS

Every manufacturer of every product lives with the constant, dread fear that someday he will awaken and find out that his product was responsible for widespread destruction, harm, suffering, and even death. What's worse, the fear is that this will occur because of no intended fault of his own, no actions on the part of evil external actors such as occurred

in the case of Tylenol, but because lurking somewhere within his product is an unknown, unforeseen but ticking time bomb. Buried somewhere
within his product is an unknown but unintended set of evil properties.
Given enough time for these properties to incubate, or for a set of en-
vironmental operating conditions vastly different from those under which
the product was designed to develop, the product becomes a lethal killer.

In September 1980, after a wave of unfavorable publicity, Proctor and
Gamble was forced to withdraw its product, Rely tampons, from the market. According to *Fortune,* "government researchers reported that over
70% of toxic-shock patients in one study had worn [the] single brand
[Rely]."[12] While, as *Fortune* reported, P & G's top scientists strongly dis-
puted the government's findings, P & G nevertheless still took a $75 mil-
lion loss on its Rely business. Although Rely accounted for less than 1
percent of P & G's total annual sales of over $10 billion, taking it off the
market still cut $0.91 off P & G's net earnings per share of $7.78.[13]

In a sense, Toxic Shock Syndrome (TSS) can be thought of as one of
the results of our undying fascination with the "bigger or more is better
syndrome." As an August 1981 article in *Fortune* put it, the menstrual
products industry got caught up in an "absorbency sweepstakes."[14]
Each new innovation by one manufacturer only spurred the others to
match or to exceed one another. The innovations also came at a time
when women welcomed the greater freedom that slimmer pads promised
and tampons that could remain inside for longer periods of time.

TSS hit at the height of this sweepstakes. However, other than an "association" with tampons in general and with P & G's Rely in particular,
no one knows for sure why tampons "cause" TSS and there is no definitive proof that they do. The best thinking of the research community is
that a Toxin produced by a bacteria, *Staphylococcus aureus,* is the underlying cause of TSS.[15] Researchers also seem convinced that the bacteria
in case are a mutant strain. Because of the longer length of time in which
they can be left in a woman's body and because of their greater absorbency, the new tampons are believed to give the bacteria a more fertile
environment in which to grow. Also not out of the question is the possi-
bility that the tampons also help the bacteria along by irritating the lin-
ing of the vagina, thus giving the bacteria easier entry into the body's
bloodstream.[16]

At this point, more than 400 lawsuits against Rely are still pending.
The first jury verdict against P & G resulted in a strange and unpredictable outcome. Both sides were judged to have lost.[17] The plaintiff who
asked for $25 million from P & G was awarded neither punitive nor com-
pensatory damages despite the fact that she suffered a bout with TSS that
allegedly nearly killed her. At the same time, the jury also ruled that
P & G was guilty of selling a defective product and that it was negligent

in putting Rely on the market. However, the court also found that P & G did not violate any of its warranties in selling Rely.

While the first lawsuit was judged a loss for both sides, P & G could be the bigger loser in the future if it is branded negligent at the outset in future trials. As *Fortune* noted, "in many states, however, negligence is irrelevant—it doesn't matter whether the manufacturers knew or could have known about TSS. The victim merely has to prove that a defect exists in the product and that the defect is causally related to the injury."[18] Proving causation one way or the other however may be what makes TSS a prime example of one of the most fundamental kinds of the unthinkable. It is bad enough that P & G had to withdraw Rely from the market and take a $75 million loss. It is also bad enough that P & G's already much bigger competitors, Kimberly Clark and Tampax, gained almost the entire 8 percent of market share that P & G lost when it went out of the business. But what may be even worst of all is that because of the emotional impact of TSS, P & G may suffer irrevocable loss of the tampon business, for a disease that one may never be able to link up with complete certainty to its product!

How can one identify the single property or set of properties from the many which compose any product as "potentially responsible" for "causing" harm? What can be done to defend one's self against guilt by "weak association," where a direct link between one's product(s) and serious harm can be neither proved nor disproved conclusively?[19]

UNWANTED COMPATIBILITY, THE EVIL OF THE PARASITE: THE CASE OF ATARI

Suppose that the foundation of your business was the image of being identified as a provider of good, clean entertainment for the entire family. Suppose also that someone made an unauthorized, "adult" or X-rated component that was compatible with your product. This unauthorized component could only be used in conjunction with your product or something equivalent to it. This happened to Atari, the well-known maker of video games and equipment.[20]

American Multiple Industries of Northridge, California, released an "adult" game cartridge called Custer's Revenge. In the "game" a naked General Custer dodges flying arrows and various obstacles to have "intercourse" (some outraged groups have contended "rape") with an Indian maiden whose hands are tied behind her back to a stake. Even in a world where one witnesses so many human tragedies and outrageous acts, and as a result one tends to become jaded or numbed to them after a time, one still has to marvel at the kind of mind that has the "imagination" to create such monstrosities, let alone the gall to call them "games" to justify their existence. As *Fortune* recently reported:

> Custer, along with Bachelor Party and Beat 'Em & Eat 'Em, will be in stores for Christmas [1982]. American Multiple's investment so far is around $1.2 million, and [American's president] expects sales this year to reach $13 million. His selling proposition may be unique, but as [he] explains it, his motive is common to all in the cartridge trade: "We're in this business to make bank deposits."[21]

While X-rated cartridges are the most appalling examples of this kind of unwarranted intrusion, they are by no means an isolated exception. The very success of both Atari and Mattel, who at one time made all of the cartridges used in their home game recorders, prompted others to exploit their exceedingly attractive market. Again as *Fortune* put it:

> Even the cleverest cartridge, provider of untold hours of amusement, consists of a humble $4 or $5 in materials: a memory chip, printed circuit board, plastic case, label, and a cardboard box to travel in. A popular cartridge fetches a splendid $16 or so for its maker and can retail for twice that much. People who own consoles typically buy five or more cartridges a year. Sales should double to around 70 million cartridges this year [1982], bringing their manufacturers over $1 billion in revenues.[22]

With such profits to be made for so little in initial investment, it is not surprising that Activision engineers, for one, learned how to "reverse engineer" Atari consoles to make them compatible with Activision cartridges. That is, by working backwards from a given piece of equipment, in this case Atari consoles, Activision engineers figured out how to make cartridges that would run on Atari machines. While Atari couldn't prevent reverse engineering from taking place, it did sue Activision for $21 million, alleging theft of trade secrets by former Atari employees who went to work for Activision. While Atari settled out of court for an unknown amount, neither the settlement nor Atari's action have kept Activision from cashing in on a fertile market.

Notice carefully that it is not the fact of piracy itself that is unthinkable. Quite the contrary. It's common all the time. It's rather the specific nature of it that is perhaps unthinkable here. Pornography is no longer a rarity in our society. Indeed it's out in the open. Our point is not to debate whether its effects are beneficial or harmful. That is not our basic concern here. What's unthinkable is that one could actually invent and market a "game" that not only depicts rape but makes it a central feature of a product that is compatible with an innocent receiving bystander.

PROJECTION, THE EVIL IN THE MIND'S EYE:
THE CASE OF PROCTER AND GAMBLE'S LOGO

Nearly every organization craves a strong logo, an outward sign to the external world that says herein lies a distinctive product of an organization with a strong sense of mission and identity. Little wonder then that organizations often spend hundreds of thousands of dollars to create a distinctive sign and often go to great lengths to prevent competitors from encroaching on their symbol space.[23] Indeed a distinctive sign or a catchy trademark and a strong culture often go hand-in-hand. Each is the accompaniment of the other.[24]

According to two of the most recent best-selling books on management,[25] Procter and Gamble is an example of one of the U.S.'s excellent companies. It is also one of the best examples of an organization with a strong culture. Supposedly one of the distinguishing marks of a strong culture and a successful organization is its unwavering commitment to the customer. The customer not only comes first in such organizations but *is* the raison d'être of the organization. P & G learned early on in its history the value of a distinctive logo in communicating its strong commitment to "listening to its customers." As Deal and Kennedy tell it:

> From the earliest days of P&G, its founding fathers always had an eye clearly fixed on what might be important to customers. One morning in 1851, William Procter noticed that a wharfhand was painting black crosses on P&G's candle boxes. Asking why this was done, Procter learned that the crosses allowed illiterate wharfhands to distinguish the candle boxes from the soap boxes. Another artistic wharfhand soon changed the black cross to a circled star. Another replaced the single star with a cluster of stars. And then a quarter moon was added with a human profile. Finally, P&G painted the moon and stars emblem on all boxes of their candles.
>
> At some later date, P&G decided that the "man in the moon" was unnecessary so they dropped it from their boxes. Immediately P&G received a message from New Orleans that a jobber had refused delivery of an entire shipment of P&G candles. Since these boxes lacked the full "moon and stars" design, the jobber thought they were imitations. P&G quickly realized the value of the "moon and stars" emblem and brought it back into use by registering it as a trademark. It was the beginning of brand name identification for P&G and the first of many times that P&G listened to its customers.[26]

Imagine the shock then one morning when P & G awoke to find that a strange religious sect had declared that P & G was in cahoots with the devil because the "man in the moon" symbol was obviously a sign of the devil.[27] After all, the "man in the moon" symbol was more than just that. It was a picture of a man wearing a "sorcerer's" cone-shaped hat with a half-moon symbol surrounded by a number of stars—clearly a sign of the devil, or at least it was for the particular religious group seeing it as that.

Such incidents are far from being isolated. Imagine the shock that Sears-Roebuck, the nation's largest retailer, received when it too was accused of being in league with the devil. According to a report on the ABC TV program "20/20," the first three digits on all of Sears's innumerable plastic credit cards were 666. As anyone who has ever had even a fleeting acquaintance with the Bible knows, the number 666 is how the devil shall be recognized!

In many, many ways this category of an unthinkable, tragic act is the most remarkable of all. It involves one of the most incredible features of the human mind, its seemingly endless ability and need to project onto other persons and even other inanimate objects some of the deepest symbolic urges which emanate from the innermost recesses of the human psyche. It's bad enough for a manufacturer to contemplate how he protects himself from the invasion of foreign, unknown, or unintended substances into his products, or even from unintended uses, but how in the world does he protect himself from the invasion of unintended *thoughts?* Foreign substances are at least material things, but thoughts?! There may be little consolation in taking action through lawsuits or in the fact of religious leaders of all persuasions coming to your aid to dispel the viciousness of the accusations.[28]

WHEN AN ENTIRE BELIEF SYSTEM COLLAPSES, THE EVIL OF BLINDNESS TO CHANGE: THE CASE OF "MONOLITHIC MOTORS"

All of us at one time or another have had the shock of seeing one or more of our cherished beliefs suddenly and unexpectedly go sour. What we took as an unshakeable truth about the world suddenly proved to be false. For instance, most of us have suffered the disappointment of betrayal. It's a bitter pill to discover that someone who was so close to us that we assumed without question, their undying credibility or loyalty could not be depended upon in a moment of real need. Similarly, many of us have experienced the crash of an investment, be it large or small. In most cases, our actions were based on an assumption that we took for granted. Lacking perfect knowledge into either the souls of men's hearts or the complex workings of a huge economic system, much of what we do is founded inevitably on the presumed truth of countless assumptions most of which we are never even aware that we are making.[29] Imagine then the shock when one or more of our assumptions comes crashing down. Even worse, imagine the greatest shock of all when every single one of the assumptions upon which our view of the world was based collapses entirely and almost overnight. Such is the predicament in which many of our most prized industries in recent years have found themselves.

A colleague of ours, James O'Toole, has recently examined the assumptions upon which one of our major industries, the automobile, was based. In a paper provocatively titled "Declining Innovation: The Failure of Success,"[30] O'Toole argues that a relatively small set of assumptions, ten in all, can be identified with the initial success of U.S. automobile companies. When those same companies, however, failed to change their assumptions in tune with the realities of the changing times, those very same assumptions were responsible for their subsequent near death, or at the very least, severe economic ill-health. Examining the assumptions of a fictitious car company called appropriately enough Monolithic Motors (M.M.), O'Toole states the case, both succinctly and well:

> The guiding principles that led to M.M.'s early success were crystalized into operating assumptions for all subsequent generations of managers.
>
> All the guiding assumptions were based on the pioneering policies that had made M.M. one of the most successful industrial organizations in the world. By repeating what had made it successful in the past, the company became even more successful. In turn, they reinforced the legitimacy of the operating assumptions. These assumptions then became unchallengeable—and unchallenged. Why challenge an idea with eternal validity? Only a fool would knock success.
>
> Alas, nothing fails like success.[31]

The basic assumptions which described M.M.'s core belief system as it entered the 1970s were as follows:

1. M.M. is in the business of making money, not cars.
2. Success comes not from technological leadership but from having the resources to quickly adopt innovations successfully introduced by others.
3. Cars are primarily status symbols. Styling is therefore more important than quality to buyers who are, after all, going to trade up every other year.
4. The U.S. car market is isolated from the rest of the world. Foreign competitors will never gain more than 15 percent of the domestic market.
5. Energy will always be cheap and abundant.
6. Workers do not have an important impact on productivity or product quality.
7. The consumer movement does not represent the concerns of a significant portion [of] the U.S. public.

8. The government is the enemy. It must be fought tooth and nail every inch of the way.
9. Strict, centralized financial controls are the secret to good administration.
10. Managers should be developed from the inside.[32]

As we all know by now, the world changed drastically in the 1970s. The environment caused the assumptions, which had served M.M. so well in the past, to be outdated, worn, and invalid. Almost overnight, their very success, their very existence was severely threatened as never before:

> Gasoline became expensive; the auto market became internationalized; the rising cost of (and time required for) retooling made it necessary to be a leader rather than a follower in the introduction of new technology; consumer values changed from styling to quality; the size of families shrunk; people could no longer afford to trade their cars in every few years; worker values and attitudes changed; successful government relations required cooperation rather than an adversarial; the few "kooks" in California who bought Volkswagens and read *Consumer Reports* [became] an important segment of the auto buying public.... By 1980 the environment had changed so thoroughly that the brilliant assumptions created by the company's founders to meet the exigencies of the environment of the 1920's were inappropriate in the radically-altered environment fifty years later.[33]

As O'Toole correctly points out, innovation, if not one's very continued existence, necessitates a continual scanning of the environment for changes, however minute, that are always occurring.[34] Even more difficult, it requires each organization to act on those changes before it is too late to take positive advantage of them. In other words, it is important to act before one is forced to backtrack from a situation one did not want to get in to begin with.

Particularly over the past two years, attention has begun to be focused on companies that are successful. The recent best seller by Peters and Waterman, *In Search of Excellence*,[35] attests to our need to reaffirm that not everything we have done as a culture is all bad. Surely it can not be the case that there are no good U.S. companies. The Japanese can not have a monopoly on truth or goodness. They can not have found the magic elixir that guarantees universal success. While it is certainly true that we are not as bad and the Japanese are not as good as we have been led to believe, it is nonetheless ironic to conclude that it may be precisely those companies which are the most successful that have the most difficulty in changing themselves in response to significant changes in the environment. The very things (that is, guiding assumptions) that bred success in the past may be the biggest barriers to change precisely when it is needed most.[36] Why change when things have gone so well in the past? Why change when things are going well in the present particularly if there are only vague signs of an approaching dark cloud?

What a topsy-turvy world indeed in which we live and which we have fashioned. Nothing may breed failure like success! How does one guard against the dangers of success? Is it any accident that in this context one is reminded of Oscar Wilde's biting and insightful words that there are two great tragedies in life: The first is not getting what you want; the second is getting it.[37] Is there anything more that one can offer the beleaguered organization than this sardonic insight?

A RECAPITULATION

The situations reported here are unfortunately no longer rare. One could go on forever expanding our preliminary list of unthinkable, tragic acts.[38] For instance, a Los Angeles *Times* editorial of January 24, 1983, reports that more than $400 billion in foreign debt is owed by the developing nations to Western banks.[39] Of this staggering amount, U.S. banks oversee $94 billion in unpaid loans. Many of the Third World and Communist nations can't even make the interest payments on their loans let alone the combined payment of principal plus interest. According to the editorial, banks seem to have no choice but to throw good money after bad in order to keep the debtors afloat. Outright failure to repay threatens the entire global economy. As a result, the debtors or lendees are literally in the position of dictating repayment terms to the lendors. The editorial asks whether we have become the prisoners of our debtors. Indeed, just identifying who the victims and the villains are in this complex game is no longer a trivial matter.

The biggest example of the "evil of the danger from within" may be the Johns-Manville asbestos case.[40] According to the investment firm of Moody's, asbestos-related liability cases could well extend into the year 2010, with the amounts of money at stake to Johns-Manville alone estimated at between $4 and $10 billion. According to the *Economist*, U.S. asbestos companies as a whole face potential claims of $120 to $150 billion from the victims of asbestos exposure.

On a more humorous note (but not to the manufacturer), one has to smile at the case of the youngster who opened up a box of Cracker Jack expecting to find a prize inside. Instead of finding the usual trinket that Cracker Jack is known for, the child in this case found a small pamphlet of "Swedish erotica on unusual sexual positions." Needless to say, neither the child's parents nor the manufacturer were amused, although the offending plant employee might have been.

With regard to the category of "the evil from without or projection," two additional cases in particular stand out. One has to do with one of the most tasteless aspects of the whole Tylenol case. The other has to do with a form of projection that is virtually nonexistent for most of us.

One of the most bizarre aspects of the Tylenol case has to do with the lot numbers that contained poisonous capsules.[41] In New Hampshire, Pennsylvania, and Rhode Island, three of the states that contain lotteries, officials had to halt betting on the numbers 2,880 and 1,910 when wagers on them reached maximum liability levels. Apparently for sizable numbers of our fellow citizens some numbers are more imbued with luck no matter how the association with luck is arrived at! In magical thinking after all, extreme evil is as much a source or sign of luck as is goodness. Who ever said that betting on a tragedy wasn't big business?

The December 22, 1982, issue of the West Virginia Martinsburg *Evening Journal* contained a story that shows that projection is not only in the eye of the beholder but sometimes it is even in the ear as well.[42] Apparently a shipment of dolls that should have gone to Hispanics on the West Coast ended up on the East Coast instead. When a cord was pulled the doll uttered a phrase that was supposed to say, "I want mommy," or "I love mommy." The dolls intended for the West Coast were naturally programmed to speak Spanish. In Spanish, the phrase for I want or I love mommy is, "Quiero a Mami." Now apparently some of the recording mechanisms got speeded up so when adults who might have purchased the doll pulled the cord, they thought they heard,"Kill mommy" instead of "I love mommy." Quite a difference! The doll manufacturers of course heard no such thing. They certainly intended no such thing. That didn't prevent a recall of the dolls nonetheless.

Finally, there is the recent case of the hot dog manufacturer, Hygrade, that makes the nationally successful brand Ball Park.[43] Hygrade had to recall 1 million franks at a cost of around 1 million dollars when customers reported finding razor blades in the product. At first the company suspected internal sabotage. That was dispelled when the company discovered, unfortunately only *after* the recall, that the reports were a hoax. They were completely fabricated. Even more bizarre than the hoaxes themselves was the finding, to the complete shock of the company, that there is nothing criminal about inserting a razor blade into a product such as a hot dog, calling the police, and claiming that the product was found in that condition! If the hoaxers had demanded money from Hygrade, that would be punishable as extortion. But the hoaxers never did this. The only crime of which they were guilty was that of filing a false police report. For this offense the perpetrators served ten days.

All of the cases reported in this chapter only touch on the topic of corporate tragedies. There may literally be no end to the different kinds of tragic, unthinkable acts that are capable of occurring in a complex society. Whether there are some systematic ways to think about and to cope with such things is therefore a matter of supreme importance. One thing however is certain: In almost all cases such acts are sufficient to get the attention of even the most blasé organization. In almost every case, a tragedy involves a considerable, or at the very least a noticeable, proportion of the organization's total revenues. For instance, in Hygrade's case, 1 million dollars was involved in a recall where annual revenues reach 8 million dollars. If a one-eighth or 12 percent loss of annual revenue in one fell swoop is not enough to get the attention of an organization that something somewhere has gone wrong in our society then perhaps nothing will. Any organization that doesn't think it has a serious problem today is perhaps so out of touch with reality that maybe it doesn't deserve to survive. We hope this is not the case.

Such tragedies do more than test a company's financial mettle. More fundamentally, they test its spirit, its will to believe in itself and its products as never before. There are strong signs that all the companies mentioned in this chapter will recover. Even so, there will always be the memory of "a dark and deep tragedy in the family's history" from which they may never fully recover.

In the rest of this book, we want to explore what has made modern organizations more susceptible to such acts and what if anything can be done to cope with them before, during, and after their occurrence. The closing lines to the *Fortune* article on the Hygrade case are a fitting note on which to end this chapter:

> Food manufacturers, in common with many other businesses, could not keep going for long without a base of trust. Hygrade, like Johnson & Johnson in its Tylenol ordeal demonstrated the value of openness and consistency with the press when trust in a product is shaken. Since destructive acts of sociopaths, when directed against companies, cannot now be prevented or even deterred by threat of punishment, they can only be planned for and perhaps coped with.[44]

In sum, this book is fundamentally how to think about and how to cope with the unthinkable, how to anticipate and to manage corporate tragedies.

NOTES

1. Thomas Moore, "The Fight to Save Tylenol," *Fortune*, November 29, 1982, pp. 44–49.
2. Ibid., p. 44.
3. Bob Wischia, "The Tylenol Disaster," *Runner's World Presents*, January 1983, pp. 4–9, and "Tylenol Chronology," *Runner's World Presents*, January 1983, p. 11.

4. Wischia, "The Tylenol Disaster," pp. 4–9.

5. Moore, *The Fight to Save Tylenol,* p. 44.

6. Ibid., p. 49.

7. Ibid.

8. Ibid.

9. William H. Reid, ed., *The Psychopath, A Comprehensive Study of Antisocial Disorders and Behaviors* (New York: Bruner/Mazel, 1978).

10. Ian I. Mitroff, Richard O. Mason, and Vincent P. Barabba, *The 1980 Census: Policy Making Amid Turbulence* (Lexington, Mass.: Lexington Press, 1983).

11. Georgie Anne Geyer, "Tylenol Murders Raise Horrifying Questions About Terrorist Methods," Vancouver, B.C. Province, 1982.

12. Pamela Sherrid, "Tampons After the Shock Wave," *Fortune,* August 10, 1981, pp. 114–29.

13. "Tampons, Not Relied On," *The Economist,* September 27, 1980, p. 100.

14. Sherrid, "Tampons," p. 115.

15. "Toxic Shock, Horror Mystery," *The Economist,* October 18, 1980, p. 42.

16. Ibid.

17. Thonda L. Rundle, "Verdict in Rely Case Could Hurt P&G Later," *Business Insurance,* March 29, 1982, pp. 25–26.

18. Sherrid, "Tampons," p. 119.

19. Sherrid, "Tampons," p. 119, and Jean L. Marx, "New Clue to the Cause of Toxic Shock," *Science* 220. (April 15, 1983):290.

20. Andrew C. Brown, "Cashing In On The Cartridge Trade," *Fortune,* November 15, 1982, pp. 125–28.

21. Ibid., p. 128.

22. Ibid., p. 125.

23. B. G. Yovovich, "In Search Of A New Corporate Label, Things Change, and The Names Don't Remain The Same," *Advertising Age,* March 7, 1983, p. M-23.

24. Terrence E. Deal and Allan A. Kennedy, *Corporate Cultures, The Rites and Rituals of Corporate Life* (Reading, Mass.: Addison-Wesley, 1982), pp. 27–28.

25. Ibid., and Thomas J. Peters and Robert H. Waterman, *In Search of Excellence, Lessons From America's Best-Run Companies* (New York: Harper and Row, 1982).

26. Deal and Kennedy, *Corporate Cultures,* pp. 27–28; see also, "Moon and Stars Trademark," available from The Procter & Gamble Company, P. O. Box 599, Cincinnati, Ohio 45201.

27. "Procter & Gamble's Symbol of Quality," The Procter and Gamble Company; see also a news release packet available from the Public Affairs Division of P & G.

28. "Procter and Gamble's Symbol of Quality," The Procter and Gamble Company; see also news release packet.

29. Richard O. Mason and Ian I. Mitroff, *Challenging Strategic Planning Assumptions* (New York: John Wiley, 1981).

30. James O'Toole, "Declining Innovation: The Failure of Success, A Summary Report of the Seventh Twenty Year Forecast Project," Center for Futures Research, Graduate School of Business, University of Southern California, Los Angeles, Calif., pp. 1–28.

31. Ibid., p. 4.

32. Ibid.

33. Ibid., p. 5.

34. Mason and Mitroff, *Challenging Strategic Planning Assumptions.*

35. Peters and Waterman, *In Search of Excellence.*

36. Mitroff, Mason, and Barabba, *The 1980 Census.*

37. John Bartlett, *Familiar Quotations,* 14th ed. (Boston: Little, Brown, 1968), p. 839.

38. "Formaldehyde: The Problem That Won't Go Away," *Changing Times,* February 1983, pp. 52–55.

39. Ernest Conine, "For Bankers, Crossed Fingers, Action Is Needed to Save World System, But Will It Be Taken?", Los Angeles *Times*, January 24, 1983, Part II, p. 5.

40. Stephen Tarnoff, "Defending Asbestos Suit Pays Off for Unarco," *Business Insurance*, December 28, 1981, pp. 38–39; Stephen Tarnoff, "Asbestos Defendants' Bond Ratings Cut," *Business Insurance*, November 1, 1982, pp. 32–33; Stephen Tarnoff, "Johns-Manville Sues M&M for Policy Gap," *Business Insurance*, January 18, 1982, pp. 3, 25; "Warning: Asbestos May Cost You More Than Money," *The Economist*, July 11, 1981, pp. 83–84; "Which Insurer Is Liable For Asbestosis Cases?", *Business Week*, November 9, 1981, pp. 30–31.

41. Wischia, "The Tylenol Disaster," pp. 4–9.

42. "Doll Shock Comes to Berkeley," *The Evening Journal*, December 22, 1982, pp. A-1, A-2.

43. Geoffrey Colvin, "Product Tampering: Lessons From A Hot Dog Maker's Ordeal," *Fortune*, March 7, 1983, pp. 77–82.

44. Ibid., p. 82.

2

Picture Shock:
Why Our Old Images of the World Don't Work Anymore

"The whole thing is premised on faith," Stockman explained. "On a belief about how the world works."[1]

"Who knows?" The world was less manageable than he had imagined; this machine had too many crazy moving parts to incorporate in a single lucid theory. The "random elements" of history—politics, the economy, the anarchical budget numbers—were out of control.[2]

William Greider,
"The Education of David Stockman"

In this chapter we begin the journey that will occupy us throughout the rest of this book. The purpose or the goal is to show how one can cope more effectively with the kinds of corporate tragedies that result from the impact of the unthinkable on any organization. Like most complex matters, how to accomplish this can not be given in a simple, neat formula or in a few quick lines. Indeed, the widespread affliction in our culture to demand quick, glib answers to complex questions is itself one of the biggest factors responsible for the increasing growth of tragic events. It takes only a single introductory chapter to state the existence of the tragic. It takes at least a whole book to learn how to cope with it intelligently.

A tragedy of any sort is always "an unwelcome visitor" in our lives.[3] It challenges our established habits and breaks our everyday routines. It threatens our basic beliefs regarding the predictability and orderliness of the world. It says that the means we have traditionally used to give definition, order, and structure to our existence no longer apply. This more than anything else helps to explain why a corporate tragedy is such a demoralizing force on any organization that has experienced its influence. Overnight, in one fell swoop, a tragedy shatters the images or

17

the pictures we all carry around in our heads regarding how the world is supposed to work.

To see this, we need to look at some basic images or pictures of the modern corporation and its relationship to the surrounding world. Doing this will not only help us in understanding why certain kinds of tragedies are more prevalent than ever in our daily lives but it will also aid us in showing in a later chapter how one can cope more effectively with them.

We believe that for our purposes three main images are sufficient to account for the multitude of ways in which the modern corporation has been viewed. In saying this, no one is more aware than we of the danger in reducing the richness of history down to three entities, no matter how strong each of them may be individually. Thus, we are not saying that there have literally been only three major conceptions of the modern corporation throughout history. Rather our contention is that three pictures are sufficient for the reader to gain a feel for the incredible complexity and unpredictability of the forces that now act on the modern corporation.

NOTE!

The images we form in our heads to make sense of the world and to describe its working are always the products of a specific historical age. Each image is thus appropriate for its age but not necessarily for succeeding ages. The phenomenon of corporate tragedies forces us to acknowledge that our earlier images of the corporation and its relationship to the surrounding world are no longer sufficient to make sense of and to cope with the world in which we now live. We may long for our earlier images with all the comfort and the security that they promised in their orderliness and simplicity, but longing will not bring back the earlier ages in which they were applicable.

The three images we want to discuss in turn are: the world as a simple machine, the world as a complex system, and the world as a complex, social network. Each implies a different relationship of the corporation to its environment and, as a result, a different way of examining the nature of the modern corporation.

THE WORLD AS SIMPLE MACHINE

The oldest image of the world that still dominates the vast majority of economic and managerial science is that of "the world as a simple machine." The classic contemporary expression of this view is found in the thinking of Milton Friedman. According to this view, the world of the modern corporation can be decomposed into three primary and distinctly separable entities: the corporation itself, stockholders, and customers (see

Figure 2-1). The reason is the oft-asserted statement that the sole purpose of management (presumably the upper echelons of the corporation) is to serve the primary party in their environment, i.e., the stockholders. The stockholders provide the initial working capital to allow the corporation to commence operations, to produce goods, and to sell them to customers. This is the sense in which the arrow going *from* the circle represented by the stockholders *to* the circle represented by the corporation is to be interpreted.

In return for necessary goods and services, the customers provide payments in the form of income to the corporation. The corporation then subtracts off from its income the costs it needs to do business and, if the difference is positive, provides a return on initial investment or ROI to the stockholders. Now of course the actual story is a lot more complicated than this, but in its essentials, this is the picture with which we are presented.

From the perspective of this particular story, all other interest groups either do not exist, do not deserve to be recognized, or are not recognized as exerting a significant influence on the corporation. At a minimum, this view assumes that the rest of the environment can be clearly differentiated and separated from the three characters in Figure 2-1. Hence, the reasons for the dotted lines around the surrounding social system.

As many writers have noted, among them notably Russell Ackoff[4] and Alvin Toffler[5], this view of the world is founded on the taken-for-granted metaphor that the world is a simple machine. As such, the metaphor derives from the industrial revolution when the entire world including man, plants, animals, and the environment was conceived of in mechanical terms.

Since by definition a machine is something which can be broken down into its separate parts, the reduction of a complex system into the

FIGURE 2-1

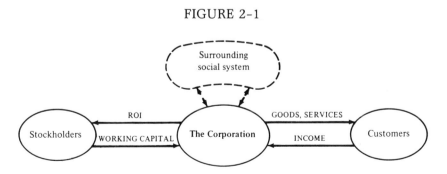

The World As Simple Machine

independent study of its individual parts was and still is the favored method of studying things from this perspective. Since a machine is also by definition something which can be objectified—it has no emotions or feelings—its working can be described in purely impersonal terms. Hence, economics was and still is a natural framework in which to describe the workings of society and organizations. More precisely one should say, the *kind* of economics we have largely developed was suited to this representation of reality, i.e., the brand of economics that recognizes only the ego or conscious components of man's psyche as a valid operating force within him and therefore views man exclusively as a rational calculating device, making all his decisions on the strict basis of benefits versus cost calculations alone. A more accurate label for this brand of economics would be the term "egonomics."

If one grants the supposition of egonomics as true of all men, then the behavior of and between individuals could also be described as a series of impersonal economic transactions. Actors merely transferred payments between them, not such intangible things as feelings or values. Or if feelings existed, they only did so by being objectified, by being measured in terms of utilities, i.e., what one was willing to sacrifice or pay for them. No wonder that this attitude set in motion an activity that continues to this day: the attempt to describe the workings of a complex economic system in terms of a series of mathematical equations or models. Further, since individual egos are supposedly separable from one another, the properties of each individual were, in principle, also separable from the rest of the system. To be sure, how individuals behaved was a function of the rest of the system, but supposedly their internal properties were not. Thus, the individual could in principle be removed from and studied in isolation from the rest of the surrounding social system.

It has come as a painful shock to those who have been brought to believe in this picture of the world that it no longer applies. Even worse, given nothing else to fall back on, they have been rendered helpless in the face of the collapse of their earlier beliefs. This is the real tragedy of the recent exposé, "The Education of David Stockman,"[6] not the fact that political shenanigans were involved in the federal budget process. What else does one expect from a process that is fundamentally political? What's news is the open revelation that the old ways of perceiving things no longer work:

> The budget politics of 1981 . . . was . . . based upon a bewildering set of numbers that confused even those, like Stockman, who produced them.
> "None of us really understands what's going on with all these numbers," Stockman confessed at one point. "You've got so many different budgets out and so many different baselines and such complexity now

in the interactive parts of the budget between policy action and the economic environment and all the internal mysteries of the budget, and there are a lot of them. People are getting from A to B and it's not clear how they are getting there. It's not clear how we got there, and it's not clear how Jones is going to get there.''

These ''internal mysteries'' of the budget process were not dwelt upon by either side, for there was no point in confusing the clear lines of political debate with a much deeper and unanswerable question: Does anyone truly understand, much less control, the dynamics of the federal budget intertwined with the mysteries of the national economy? Stockman pondered this question occasionally, but since there was no obvious remedy, no intellectual construct available that would make sense of this anarchical universe, he was compelled to shrug at the mystery and move ahead. ''I'm beginning to believe that history is a lot shakier than I ever thought it was,'' he said, in a reflective moment. ''In other words, I think there are more random elements, less determinism and more discretion, in the course of history than I ever believed before. Because I can see it.''[7]

Nowadays it is easy to laugh at the naïveté if not the simplemindedness of the notion of the world as a simple machine. It is important to understand nonetheless the basis of its enormous appeal. No picture survives for long if it doesn't have something going for it. If we keep vividly in our minds that it is an enormous simplification to reduce all of history down to three great waves as Alvin Toffler does, then we can use Toffler's simplification nonetheless to help us understand the appeal that a picture that captures the spirit of its time generates. Thus, the first great wave of history that mankind passed through was that of the agricultural revolution. It took mankind ten thousand years or so to learn how to tame nature. As our daily experience constantly shows, the taming or the war against nature is never finally won. There are always crop failures due to floods, frosts, pests, and so on. There are always catastrophic events such as earthquakes to be dealt with. Nevertheless, in terms of modern agricultural methods, the war against nature is nothing compared to earlier times. From the standpoint of earlier periods, nature has been conquered.

Around 300 years ago, a second great wave passed over Western civilization. It was as great in its consequences as the first wave was. It was the industrial revolution. Whereas the victory of the first wave was against an opponent not of man's making, i.e., of an opponent outside of him—Mother Nature—the victory of the second wave was against an opponent of man's own direct making, machines. If the war of the first wave was against nature herself, then the war of the second wave was against a part of man's nature, ''artifactual nature.''

By the terms "victory" and "war," we mean that the conquering of nature and of machines freed men from their enslavement to them. As a result of the victories over nature and machines, very few men were required to produce the food necessary to feed an entire civilization. As John Naisbett points out in his best-selling book, *Megatrends,*[8] we are on the brink of a situation similar to that which occurred around the early 1900s. Whereas a majority of the population was engaged in agriculture around the turn of the century, only 4 to 7 percent of the population are needed to grow the food we now require. Naisbett and others project that only 4 to 7 percent will be required to build the cars and machines we need today.

The point is that the victories over nature and machines were not only so demanding but so profound in their influences on our lives that it is no surprise that each wave implanted firmly in our minds' eyes a fundamental perspective from which man viewed the entire world. Thus, at the height of the second wave the world was not just metaphorically conceived of as a machine. It was not just thought of as a machine. It *was* literally a machine.[9]

The language of warfare, of opponents, victors and victories over nature will not have escaped the reader. Because of its aggressiveness, we want to make clear that this language does not represent our view of man and his relation to nature. Needless to say, many people today find the language of a "war against nature" highly offensive. They charge, and with good reason, that conceiving of nature solely as an abstract, impersonal "thing" to be used, to be conquered, or to be thought of in purely economic terms is itself responsible for much of our callous attitude toward the environment.

Few have stated better the criticism toward those who think of the corporation and the environment solely in economic terms than Alvin Toffler. Those who defend the corporation as an economic entity persist in thinking of it in language that was appropriate for the "second-wave"; Toffler on the other hand points out that the critics of the corporation criticize it from the perspective of the newly emerging "third-wave." The two perspectives are talking about two very different pictures of the corporation:

> Throughout the Second Wave era corporations have been seen as economic units, and the attacks on them have essentially focused on economic issues. Critics assailed them for underpaying workers, overcharging customers, forming cartels to fix prices, making shoddy goals, and a thousand other economic transgressions. But no matter how violent, most of these critics accepted the corporation's self-definition: they shared the view of the corporation as an inherently economic institution.

Today's corporate critics start from a totally different premise. They attack the artificial divorce of economics from politics, morality and the other dimensions of life. They hold the corporation increasingly responsible, not merely for its economic performance but for its side effects on everything from air pollution to executive stress. Corporations are thus assailed for asbestos poisoning, for using poor populations as guinea pigs in drug testing, for distorting the development of the non-industrial world, for racism and sexism, for secrecy and deception. They are pilloried for supporting unsavory regimes or political parties, from the fascist generals in Chile and the racists in South Africa to the Communist party in Italy.

What is at issue here is not whether such charges are justified—all too often they are. What is far more important is the concept of the corporation they imply. For the Third Wave brings with it a rising demand for a new kind of institution altogether—a corporation no longer responsible simply for making a profit or producing goods but for simultaneously contributing to the solution of extremely complex ecological, moral, political, racial, sexual, and social problems.

Instead of clinging to a sharply specialized economic function, the corporation, prodded by criticism, legislation, and its own concerned executives, is becoming a multipurpose institution.[10]

THE WORLD AS A COMPLEX SYSTEM

Around the 1950s, the picture or image of the world as a simple machine, which for so long had dominated the imagination of Western culture as a result of the extreme influence of the industrial revolution, seriously began to crumple. The science of cybernetics and other methods for describing complex systems with intricate interdependencies between their components were developed.

With these developments, it could no longer be denied that the world was a complex system of interconnected elements, not a simple machine of largely independent entities. The sheer reality of what was going on in the surrounding environment could no longer be denied as well. It was only a matter of time before this realization spread to that of organizations and institutions (see Figure 2–2). The recognition dawned that the modern corporation was increasingly acted upon by a growing number and constantly shifting set of multiple players in a complex system. This broader set of players can be called *stake*holders. In contrast to the single class *stock*holders, still important to be sure, *stake*holders are *all* those vested interest groups, parties, associations, institutions, and individuals who exert a hold and a claim on modern organizations. Stakeholders are all those who either affect or who are affected by an organization and its policies (i.e., its behavior).

FIGURE 2-2

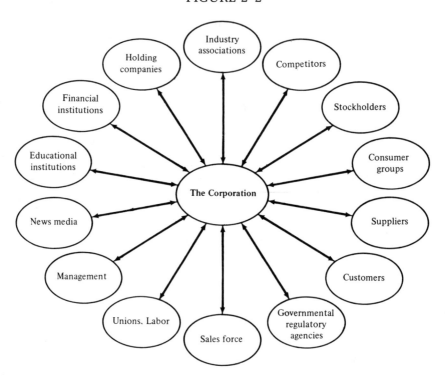

The World As A Complex System

It is important to appreciate that this view of the world differs sharply from Figure 2-1. It not only contains more parties which potentially affect the corporation, but the interrelationships between them are also very different as well. As to the first difference, the modern corporation no longer has any choice but to recognize that it must contend with a larger set of forces external to it than ever before. This is the case whether it likes or agrees with those forces or not. As the case of Monolithic Motors (M.M.) in Chapter 1 shows, all too many organizations prefer to engage in a game called 'Blame the Stakeholder' for its woes (in the case of M.M. it was blame the government) rather than deal seriously with the fact that the world in which they now operate has changed dramatically. While blaming the stakeholder might be emotionally satisfying to the participants in a corporation, it is no help whatsoever in dealing with the real world. When it comes to dealing with reality, practitioners are often little better than academics even though practitioners like to believe they are.

As to the second difference, in "the world as a complex system" picture, in principle none of the stakeholders can be described independently from the entire system of which they are a part. The properties (e.g., the behavior) of each stakeholder are not self-contained. What each stakeholder does and is like affects all other stakeholders and in turn is affected by all other stakeholders. Different stakeholders not only influence more and more on the behavior of one another but increasingly they also intrude more deeply into the internal behavior of all stakeholders. What the stakeholders external to the organization are like affects more and more what the stakeholders internal to an organization are like. For example, what IBM is like and does in the personal computer field affects what Apple does and is like and vice versa.

An even more apt metaphor for this picture is that of "the world as an organism." To take a simple example, the heart and the eye neither function nor exist separately from the brain or the rest of the body, i.e., the whole system of which they are a part. A human being strictly speaking is not an organization, i.e., a system whose "parts" have an independent existence or will of their own like the employees of a corporation do. Rather, a human being only exists as a whole entity. The individual cannot be reduced to the sum of its parts without thereby losing a vital sense of the total person. For instance, the will or the purpose of a person is not located in either the brain, the eye, or the heart. Rather, it resides in the whole of the person. Furthermore, even separate human beings are nonetheless dependent upon the larger social system for their initial existence, education, sustenance, beliefs, values, etc. Philip Slater says it well:

> It has taken more than a century for Western medicine to rediscover what witch doctors and shamans have known all along: (1) that a disease occurs in the whole organism, not, as in a machine, in one defective part; and (2) that every organism is organically related to others, and to the total environment, and hence any "cure" that does not take account of these relationships is likely to be ephemeral. What we stigmatize as magic is scientific inasmuch as it teaches the wholeness and interconnectedness of living forms. Scientific medicine, on the other hand, is irrational in that it treats the organism as if it were a machine, disconnected from its surroundings and internally disconnectable.[11]

Every one of the cases that were discussed in Chapter 1 could be used to illustrate the extreme interconnectedness between stakeholders in today's world. For instance, the January 9, 1981 issue of the Los Angeles *Times* reported that the Tylenol case "cost federal, state, and local governments well over $3 million."[12] Thousands of hours were consumed by law enforcement officials in tracking down leads all over the country related to the poisonings however tenuous a lead might be. The Food and

Drug Administration alone was reported to have spent over $2 million in testing capsules and in investigating deaths and illnesses.

In a highly interconnected and complex world, no single stakeholder possesses all of the necessary skills and resources to go it entirely alone. Every single stakeholder is dependent upon countless other stakeholders to share a critical part of its burdens. In the case of Tylenol the only way in which this would not have been true was if McNeil and its parent company J & J had the necessary resources to train and maintain their own national police force! That would surely have cost McNeil and J & J more than $3 million. Indeed, nothing in the popular press of which we are aware has been reported on which percent if any of the $3 million McNeil and J & J were obligated to pay back to state and government agencies for the assistance they received.

For a different case, consider the billions in dollars that the makers of asbestos are liable for. The victims of the chronic lung disease asbestosis naturally claim that the manufacturers are directly responsible for payment because they did not warn them of the dangers in applying asbestos.[13] For just this very reason, almost all manufacturers carry liability insurance. However, in spite of this, or rather because of it, a thorny issue arises. Since asbestosis is a disease which develops over decades, and since most asbestos manufacturers have had more than one insurance carrier over this period, which one should be held liable for payment now?

As one could expect, some of the insurance companies have argued that the liability belongs to those carriers that had the policy when the disease first became evident. Others still naturally argue that all of the companies that were ever involved during the time period that a victim was exposed to asbestos should share in the cost of liability payments. The manufacturers of asbestos of course like the latter policy because it gives them more coverage. It spreads the damage over more carriers. This is critical since the cost of even just a few claims that could be awarded to victims could very quickly exhaust the amounts of policy coverage with any single carrier. One asbestos manufacturer, Johns-Manville, has even instigated a suit against its insurance broker for failing "to put together an insurance package that would fully cover [its] asbestos claims."[14]

Since the number of potential asbestos cases is so great—estimates range between 50,000 and 60,000 of those who will be affected by the disease between now and the year 2000—it appears that neither the manufacturers nor the insurance carriers alone, or even together for that matter, could meet the total cost of all claims. Some parties have therefore suggested that another stakeholder should be involved to help share the cost, the federal government. However as one commentator on legal matters observed, "Congress may not have much truck with an industry that has been killing people, albeit unknowingly, for the past 50 years."[15]

Before we leave this section, it should be noted that "the world as complex system" picture shares some features in common with the first picture, "the world as simple machine." Both view the interactions between stakeholders as largely rational. That is, parties are governed by their self-interests which they are presumed to know. As a result, they engage one another in a series of rational calculations as to their comparative bargaining advantage over one another. The transactions or exchanges between stakeholders are largely conceived to be economic and political; in short, dollars and power. Once again we are dealing with the conception of man as a rational calculating machine. Only in this case, this conception is broadened potentially to include all of the actors in a complex system. The term that best describes this view is "syste-nomics" rather than economics.

② SYSTE-NOMICS

THE WORLD AS COMPLEX SOCIAL NETWORK

Figure 2-3, "the world as a complex social network," presupposes the existence of Figure 2-2, "the world as a complex system." Indeed, it was out of Figure 2-2 that Figure 2-3 developed. We even doubt that Figure 2-3 could have existed without the prior existence of Figure 2-2.

Figure 2-3 adds a number of things that Figure 2-2 does not contain. First, it adds a number of additional stakeholder characters that Figure 2-2 on the whole is oblivious to. These additional characters derive from the sociopathic behavior that has been directed toward corporations as was described in Chapter 1. For instance, the placing of poison in Tylenol vividly demonstrates that if the term "stakeholder" is confined to the parties shown in Figure 2-2 (suppliers, sales people, etc.), then it is far too benign to capture the full nature of the environment in which business now operates. The traditional concept of stakeholders is too limited to capture the range of evil and bizarre characters that now potentially affect the modern corporation.

For the most part, the stakeholders indicated in Figure 2-2 represent the impact of impersonal institutional forces external to the corporation on it. These forces are not wrong and Figure 2-2 is not thereby wrong in its entirety. It is merely incomplete, seriously so.

First, Figure 2-3 adds another set of stakeholders to Figure 2-2 who emanate from some of the deepest and darkest impulses that are rooted in man's psyche. More than we like to acknowledge, evil and violent impulses still reside in the deepest and most ancient part of our minds. We

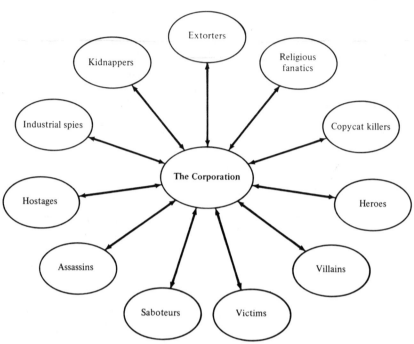

The World As A Complex Social Network

may like to think we have tamed external nature but we still have a long way to go in understanding and in taming our internal nature.

Second, Figure 2-3 is meant to indicate that all of the stakeholders in Figures 2-2 and 2-3 are potentially in contact with one another. When men either individually or in institutions interact with one another, they do more than merely engage in impersonal economic transactions. Man is much more than a mere economic calculating machine. He possesses more than an ego, a conscious mind. As Freud and Jung taught us, man also possesses a set of deeper and darker forces that operate within him and regarding which he is not conscious of and hence which operate outside the realm of our everyday awareness.

Whenever any two people or institutions interact with one another they do more than merely exchange goods, services, utilities, etc. They do this, to be sure. However, they also exchange something far deeper. They form mental images of one another. They project their hopes, their fears, their dreams, wishes, doubts, worries, joys, and anxieties on to one another. For instance, the recent case of Hitachi's attempt to steal secrets from IBM is a gold mine from a psychoanalyst's standpoint.[16] It shows that whenever two competitors interact, they form a distorted picture of one another. They inevitably see the other as more evil than the other really is; or stronger, wiser, braver, etc.

Man is thus complex not only because he engages in impersonal economic transactions but because at the very same time he also engages in interpersonal transactions that are emotionally loaded.

Thus once again, it is not so much that Figure 2–2 is wrong per se as much as it is seriously incomplete. At a minimum there is potentially a *double line* of influence (economic and psychodynamic) between each and every stakeholder in Figures 2–2 and 2–3. Man is complex because both at the conscious and the unconscious level he engages in transactions across very different levels of social reality simultaneously. More often than not he is totally unaware that he is even doing this.

One of the strong implications of this way of thinking is that at present we have no truly adequate theory of economics. Current economic theory is largely a theory of transactions which hold only at the level of the ego, i.e., conscious reality. When it comes to the ways in which the other aspects of man's complex psyche conduct transactions, we have no theory of economics that is based on the deeper aspects of the psyche.

If we lack a proper theory of economics, we do not lack for other concepts that make it possible to understand today's society. Philip Slater and Daniel Yankelovich[17] both make the point that the United States today is a network, it is not a community.

> Urban and suburban Americans do not live in communities, they live in networks. A network is an address book [extended in space and time]—a list of people who may have little in common besides oneself. Each network has only one reference point that defines it. No two people have the same precise network. This means that everyone controls her own social milieu, and if she likes can subsist entirely on interpersonal candy bars. The persons in her network do not all know each other, so *she is never forced to integrate the disparate sides of herself but can compartmentalize them in disconnected relationships* [underscoring ours].
>
> A true community [, on the other hand,] is like an ecological system where one species' waste is another species' sustenance, like the oxygen-carbon dioxide exchange between plants and animals. What one extrudes, the other seeks. *The full range of human emotionality and behavior can thus be realized in some form or another* [underscoring ours].[18]

What Slater and a host of other writers make clear is that while they are not perfect in any sense, communities are more likely to contain the evil and dark sides of our nature than are networks. In a community like a family we are forced at some point to come to grip with our evil sides. A community is a conversation with the many voices and the many sides of our personalities that compose the vast range of the human condition. Networks almost exist for the very express purpose of avoiding communication with those persons who represent those sides of our personalities we do not wish to acknowledge.

The impact of the distinction between a network and a community struck the first author with force during a conference he was attending in 1982. The conference, which was sponsored by the National University of Mexico, was entitled "How Is Mexico Going to Feed Its Population in the Year 2000?", a subject which is of considerable interest to Third-World countries. As is usual, the conference dragged on with the typical banalities one finds at such events. The typical parade of scientific experts neatly partitioned the whole problem into separate, disconnected parts so that each of them could get their hands around the bits they were comfortable in dealing with. As a result, the conversation soon degenerated into a discussion of improving food yields per acre, lowering the costs of production, etc. In short, the discussion moved to the conception of society as one big disconnected machine.

It was at this point that Russell Ackoff entered the discussion. Ackoff is a systems thinker who has worked with Mexican society for many years, and since he is not one to blunt his words, he said that the conference was a complete sham and a waste of time. Everyone in the room knew that Mexican society was riddled with four basic problems and that unless these problems were met head on, the best and the most rational scientific solutions to the food problem would be absolutely stifled before they even got off the ground. The four problems Ackoff stated were: corruption, bureaucracy, patronage, and patriarchy.

Every one of these problems was the real problem facing Mexican society. The failure of Mexico to feed its citizens was just another set of symptoms of the underlying problem. For instance, consider corruption. Corruption is a terrible disease not merely because it drains off needed economic resources from a society and distributes them wrongly, but because far more deeply it destroys the will of a country to believe in itself. It makes an absolute joke of rational problem solving. Everyone knows that nothing will really be accomplished.

Ackoff went on to argue that the Mexicans needed to abandon the fatalistic grip in which the four problems held them. He outlined some promising experiments being conducted in Mexico by Mexicans themselves that showed that they did not have to live in the inevitable grip of these four deadly social diseases.

Ackoff's remarks jarred the first author's thinking. Although no society is ever free from corruption, we in the United States do not experience it at the same level of demoralization. (Although, there is nothing in principle to prevent us from experiencing it if certain industries got out of hand, e.g., the extreme manipulation of paper profits to the extreme benefit of the very few.) Since the Tylenol experience was still fresh, the thought also occurred that instead of "corruption" we are more vulnerable to "disruption." Indeed, isn't it the point that while communities and networks are both susceptible to all social diseases, a network by definition is more susceptible to disruption at a distance?

To return to our main theme of the extreme interdependency and contamination of all stakeholders with regard to one another, we are forced to acknowledge that we live in a world where the actions of a madman are no less infectious on the emotions of a general population than those of a saint. How else are we to interpret the wave of cyanide threats that followed the poisoning of Tylenol? The January 25, 1983 issue of the Los Angeles *Times*[19] reported that National Guard troops had to haul in water to 133,000 Louisiana residents when copycat cyanide threats left them without drinkable water. As in the case of the hot dogs in Chapter 1, the threats appeared to be hoaxes. Nonetheless, authorities had no choice but to bring in fresh water supplies at considerable expense.

At present there is no theory of economics that incorporates all of the forces that we have been talking about in the last two sections. It is no longer sufficient to pretend man is a rational calculating machine. It's a shame we don't have such a revised conception of economics because we need one more than ever.

CONCLUDING COMMENTS

Engage in a little thought experiment. Line up the three figures in this chapter against the events described in Chapter 1. It is quickly seen that only the picture of the world as a complex social network is capable of accounting for the kinds of forces impacting on the modern corporation that give rise to the tragic series of events described in Chapter 1.

It should also be painfully obvious that as it stands the third picture is not an explanation of the unthinkable. It only *names* the generic types of rational and bizarre characters that now affect the modern corporation. It does not specify in detail the particular properties of specific people who commit such acts. Nor does it direct us how to cope with tragedies before, during, and after their occurrence. But then this chapter is only the first step of building toward a procedure for coping. The main message of this chapter is that our old pictures of the world are no longer adequate even at the gross level of analysis to identify the types of characters who influence the modern corporation. They're even worse at the detailed level as we show in a later chapter.

Finally, we can not leave this chapter without mentioning two more examples of the unthinkable. These examples reveal that evil is a two-way street. We would be remiss in our discussion if we ignored the evil that is committed by organizations on society as well.

The first case concerns reports in *Time* and other mass media publications to the effect that Dow Chemical Company scientists engaged in a discussion with representatives from rival firms "to keep discoveries about [the] perils [of the family of chemical agents known as dioxin] from exploding into a public scandal, which could have brought a new outcry for governmental regulation of the chemical industry."[20] Dow's behavior is also another classic example of the game "Fix the Blame on Some Other Stakeholder But Us."

The fact that Dow conspired to keep dioxin's lethal effects from being known came to light as a part of a legal action instigated on behalf of 20,000 Vietnam veterans, their widows, and children against Dow and other producers of Agent Orange. Both dioxin and Agent Orange were used to defoliate the jungles of Vietnam; hence U.S. soldiers were exposed to it as well as their Vietnamese counterparts. According to *Time,* "the suit charges that the dioxin contained in Agent Orange caused cancer and other ailments among the soldiers and genetic effects in their children. Dow has resolutely denied charges."

Other scientists stoutly disagree with Dow. To them, dioxin is extremely harmful. Supposedly "even concentrations as low as 5 parts per trillion can cause birth defects, cancer, and other serious illness in laboratory animals. [And]. . . 112 of 130 residents tested in Imperial, MO, near dioxin contaminated Times Beach, showed abnormalities in blood, liver, or kidney functions."

Finally there is the case of a California crematorium.[21] In a "lawsuit that has attracted national attention," two sisters charge that "their brother's body was cremated with several others, leaving the survivors with what [one of the sisters] describes as a box full of 'God knows whose ashes.' " If this wasn't bad enough, the language that the L. A. *Times* reported that has been used to describe the cremation business certainly was:

> Almost unheard of 10 years ago, the cremation business—or the "bake and shake crowd" as it is sometimes called—has become a significant part of the $6.4 billion funeral industry.

How in the face of such events can we cling any longer to our old pictures of the world? Persistence in our old pictures is like forcing Columbus to describe the world as flat when he knows it is a globe. It just doesn't fit anymore.

NOTES

1. William Greider, "The Education of David Stockman," *Atlantic Monthly*, December 1981, p. 29.

2. Ibid., p. 54.

3. This phrase is taken from a poem by Dana Mitroff, age 14, "Jealousy: An Unwelcome Visitor." Her father gratefully acknowledges her welcome presence in his life.

4. Russell L. Ackoff, *Creating the Corporate Future* (New York: John Wiley, 1981).

5. Alvin Toffler, *The Third Wave* (New York: William Morrow, 1980); see also Daniel Bell, *The Winding Passage* (New York: Basic Books, 1980), for a more profound analysis.

6. Greider, "Education of David Stockman," p. 29.

7. Ibid., pp. 38-39.

8. John Naisbett, *Megatrends* (New York: Warner, 1982).

9. Bell, *The Winding Passage*.

10. Toffler, *The Third Wave*, pp. 251-52.

11. Philip Slater, *Earthwalk* (New York: Anchor/Doubleday, 1974), pp. 29-30.

12. "The Nation," Los Angeles *Times*, January 9, 1981, p. 2.

13. "Which Insurer Is Liable for Asbestosis Cases?", *Business Week*, November 9, 1981, pp. 30-31.

14. Stephen Tarnoff, "Johns-Manville Sues M&M for Policy Gap," *Business Insurance*, January 18, 1982, pp. 3, 25.

15. "Warning: Asbestosis May Cost You More Than Money," *The Economist*, July 11, 1981, pp. 83-84.

16. David B. Tinnin, *"Espionage,* How IBM Stung Hitachi," *Fortune*, March 7, 1983, pp. 50-56.

17. Slater, *Earthwalk*, pp. 15-16; and Daniel Yankelovich, *New Rules, Searching for Self-Fulfillment in a World Turned Upside Down* (New York: Bantam, 1982).

18. Slater, *Earthwalk*, pp. 15-16.

19. "Cyanide Threats Rise in Louisiana," Los Angeles *Times*, January 25, 1983, p. 6.

20. *"Environment,* Dioxin Puts Dow on the Spot," *Time*, May 2, 1983, p. 62; Denise Grady, *"Environment,* The Dioxin Dilemma," *Discover*, May 1983, pp. 78-84.

21. Carol McGraw, *"Last Indignity?* Cremation: Boom Brings Controversy," Los Angeles *Times*, April 13, 1983, pp. 1, 24.

3

The Failure of Education:
If They Can't Be Radically Reformed, Then Business Schools Should Be Abolished

In physics and in chemistry, . . .recognition is based chiefly on the judgment of your peers. But in economics and psychology, what you really recognize is the impact on the laity. That's why the stature of a great psychologist can't depend on the judgment of peers, because they'll choose somebody who fed sex hormones to tapeworms and turned them into lesbians. That may have big scientific interest, but it has not the slightest impact on the world.

Peter Drucker[1]

At best, the current system of education prepares young people for preexisting jobs in high-volume, standardized production. Some students are sorted into professional ranks and trained in the manipulation of abstract symbols. Others are prepared for lower-level routine tasks in production or sales. Few students are taught how to work collaboratively to solve novel real-world problems—the essence of flexible-system production.

Robert Reich[2]

IF ALL THE BUSINESS SCHOOLS WERE ELIMINATED

One of the major theses of this book is that the tragic acts committed against corporations that we have described are the result of a number of prominent features of modern society. These features not only interact with one another repeatedly but behave in an unpredictable manner. In brief, the tragedies we have described are made possible by the nature of modern society. By saying this we do not believe in conspiracy theories. On the other hand, we do not also believe that such tragedies are a random, accidental feature of modern society. A number of prominent features combine to make such tragedies more likely in today's world.

We continue our examination of these features in this chapter. In the last chapter, we argued that both the sheer complexity and the number of the forces now acting on the modern corporation make it more possible for the corporation to be blind-sided by forces of which it is not aware, let alone of which it is not in control. In this chapter, we wish to add another set of features which contribute to our growing inability to cope with the unthinkable. These features are due to the nature of modern education, or more accurately, the nature of modern *miseducation*.

In a bluntly written and insightful article, Dr. William V. Muse, currently vice chancellor for academic programs for Texas A & M University and formerly dean of the Business School at the same institution, asks: "If all the business schools in the country were eliminated...would anyone notice?"[3] Of his own admission, Dr. Muse has a recurring fantasy where the answer that repeatedly comes to him is, "No."

The reasons for his answer are of course the important thing. They indicate why going to almost any one of the current business schools in the country is probably the very worst thing one could do in preparation for coping with corporate tragedies. Whatever instincts one had in thinking about tragic events before entering a business school are either systematically squelched or extinguished by a deliberate program of miseducation as to what management is really all about.

To understand the what and why of the curriculum of business schools today, it is necessary to go back to the early 1960s. Around that time, two extremely influential reports which were highly critical of business school education appeared.[4] The reports pointed out that business schools were little more than vocational dumping grounds. They provided little in the way of instruction other than crude, nonrigorous, highly specific descriptions of particular businesses. There was little if any generalization across many businesses to formulate a set of general principles that could apply to many situations.

These criticisms of business school hit exactly on the mark. For this and other reasons, they fell on highly receptive ears. As a result, the leadership of business schools took them seriously. They went systematically about the task of correcting things. And to a significant extent they did. Indeed, as we saw in the case of Monolithic Motors in Chapter 1, the very success of business schools in changing the appalling state of business education in the 1960s is partly responsible for the current "failure of success" of business schools. They do an extremely poor job of preparing people in coping with the world of the 1980s.

Since in the 1960s as now, the departments on university campuses which are highest in academic prestige and status are the liberal arts and sciences, business schools intentionally set out to emulate them. If the liberal arts and sciences did pure research and scholarship, then business schools would do likewise. To accomplish this, business schools hired newly accredited Ph.D.s from prestigious universities who had been trained in the so-called "pure" (i.e., untainted by practical application) sciences and academically respectable disciplines, e.g., computer science, economics, industrial engineering, mathematics, political science, psychology, sociology. As a result, the academic research respectability of business schools went up enormously. As Muse correctly notes, "Only the most hardened anti-business faculty members [on university campuses] would raise questions today about [the] legitimacy [of a business school] or our right to a place on a college campus."[5]

There were of course a number of other important consequences of these actions. For one, business school faculty members began to form a closed society, or in Philip Slater's terms, they formed a network. They wrote for each other in arcane, academic journals on esoteric topics. They hired others in their own self-image. They thus insured their cloning.

A Ph.D. straight out of graduate school who had never in his or her own life even been near a real-life business organization, let alone set foot in one, could teach, write, and do research on business and management. While they thus achieved greater prestige in their own network, they increasingly lost touch with the business community and the world at large. Intentionally or unintentionally, they shut out from the halls of academia the very reality they were supposedly in the business of studying. Since the greatest prestige tended to accrue to those who could publish findings of their research in the most obtuse, usually mathematical, language, over time the "best" research was judged to be that which could be understood by the fewest numbers of one's colleagues. *Esoteric* knowledge or communication to the fewest number of persons in the network was valued a hundred times over *exoteric* knowledge or communication to the largest and most diverse numbers of persons in the wider community. Solipsism, or the most extreme emphasis on introverted communication, became generally prized as a sign of higher knowledge. Narrowness became an unwritten rule of the game. Woe unto them who attempted to communicate to the masses (i.e., the community) in direct, simple language in popular journals or who attempted to relate different fields of knowledge to one another.

Lest we be accused of exaggerating, listen to one of the most distinguished members of the economic profession, Lester Thurow, describe the narrowness of education in economics:

The discipline of economics, is on its way to becoming a guild. Members of a guild, as we know, tend to preserve and advance traditional theories rather than try to develop new ways of thinking and doing things to solve new problems. The equilibrium price-auction view of the world is a traditional view with a history as old as that of economics itself: the individual is asserted to be a maximizing consumer or producer within free supply-demand markets that establish an equilibrium price for any kind of goods or service. This is an economics blessed with an intellectual consistency, and one having implications that extend far beyond the realm of conventional economic theory. It is, in short, also a political philosophy, often becoming something approaching a religion.

Price-auction economics is further blessed because it can assume mathematical form—it can work hand in glove with calculus. Expression in mathematics imparts to the theory a seeming rigor and internal strength. But that rigor easily degenerates into scholarly rigor mortis, as mathematical facility becomes more important to the profession than a substantive understanding of the economy itself. To express an idea mathematically gives it the illusion of unassailable truth and also makes it utterly incomprehensible to anyone untutored in mathematics. Then, too, young scholars aspiring to the profession are required to demonstrate a technical virtuosity in math before they are even considered eligible. By analogy, once the Confucian scholars of ancient China passed a very complicated set of entrance examinations, they used the same examinations to keep others out. Both then and now, all honor is reserved for those who can explain current events in terms of "The Theory," while anyone trying to develop new theories to explain recent developments is regarded with suspicion at best. In economics today, "The Theory" has become an ideology rather than a set of working hypotheses used to understand the behavior of the economy found in the real world.[6]

All of this of course had some rather portentous implications for the graduates of business schools and the organizations which employed them. Since one of the prime characteristics of complex business problems is that they do not respect the ways in which man has organized knowledge, business schools became increasingly irrelevant to the complex problems of the real world. In the real world, the human and the technical "aspects" of problems exist side by side. Any attempt to pull these aspects apart or to isolate them means that one is no longer working on the same original problem.

As a result, business schools had less and less to say to the complexities that practitioners faced daily. Russell L. Ackoff may have said it best of all: "Nature is not organized in the same way that universities are." To which we would add, "but you damn well wouldn't know it by looking at the typical university catalogue."

THE BEST EDUCATIONAL SYSTEM FOR THE
EXERCISES OF THE PAST

In many ways the fault does not lie with business schools but with the things they were attempting to mimic. To understand the condition to which business schools had come, it is necessary to appreciate that they were trying to emulate a form of education that was appropriate only for the world of the industrial revolution, or as we described it in the last chapter, the world viewed as a simple machine. In that picture, the world could be decoupled into separate parts. Thus the moral, political, and social aspects of problems could be legitimately decoupled into their distinct, separate features. It was thus appropriate for that time or that model of the universe to organize the university into separate, nonoverlapping disciplines as much as was possible.

Furthermore, since a machine is in principle capable of being completely described, it was appropriate to seek for complete knowledge of things. Indeed, knowledge wasn't knowledge unless it could be both complete and certain.

In order to instill this philosophy into students, the primary mode of delivering knowledge became the textbook. Now one of the appealing features of textbooks is that they do not present problems. They present exercises. There is a vast and important difference between the two.

Exercises have one and only one correct answer. Problems generally do not. Exercises have one and generally only one correct formulation of the issue at hand. Problems do not. For instance, if someone tells you to solve the simple algebraic equation $X + 5 = 11$ where X is an unknown amount of dollars which when added to $5 or a known amount equals a total of eleven dollars, then there is indeed one and only one correct answer for X, i.e., $6. However, if someone asks you to formulate a strategy for snatching Monolithic Motors from the clutches of the "failure of success," there are likely to be as many different perceptions of the problem as there are stakeholders who influence M.M.

In the "world as a simple machine," problems and their associated solutions were presumed to be constant for all parties or what we have called stakeholders. In the world "as a complex system" and "complex social network," problems and their solutions are variable. What's an acceptable problem and a solution depends upon the particular stakeholder whose ox is being gored.

A classic example is the case of Johns-Manville that we discussed in the last chapter. Johns-Manville would naturally like as many different insurance carriers as possible to share in the burden of handling the enormous costs of asbestosis cases. Some of the insurance carriers would obviously prefer not to do this. To put it mildly, the various parties do not share the same perception of the problem.

Because exercises generally admit of one and only one correct answer, the criterion for judging success in *solving exercises* (the production of a single, absolutely correct answer) became the unconscious standard for judging success in *managing problems*. An exercise in principle once solved stays solved. A problem in principle does not. A problem changes over time. For instance, the definition of inflation is not the same for all stakeholders for all time.

The attainment of *certainty* is a valid objective in solving exercises; e.g., one produces the single, exact X for which $X + 5 = 11$; once one has this X one knows for sure that there is no other X that will work. A problem on the other hand requires us to manage and to tolerate *uncertainty*. There is no longer a single exact X that gives the correct answer to the problem because unlike an exercise, we are not given the single definitive statement of the problem by a higher, outside, objective authority or the writer of a textbook who is supposed to be above the fray.

There are no definitive, impersonally objective, textbook writers of the problems of society. Each stakeholder has his own version of society's problems. Learning how to manage different views of a problem and understanding why different stakeholders have different views thereby becomes more important than solving any single view and pretending it is the solution for all views.

How to do this is the subject of later chapters. As such, it is a critical component in coping with problems of the magnitude and nature of corporate tragedies. For now, we merely wish to make the point that the form of education that served so well in the past is no longer applicable *in its entirety* for today's problems. It may still be necessary, perhaps more so than ever, to learn how to solve exercises, but it is no longer sufficient. For this reason, we view the recent clamor over the decline of U.S. education with very mixed feelings.[7] True, the scores of American children on standardized tests (exercises!) need to be brought up to snuff. Our nation is probably behind that of other competitor nations on how our students score on math, science, and technology. *But,* while absolutely necessary, this is in itself no longer sufficient. Writing in a recent issue of *Esquire,* Frank Rose said it well:

> Technology is applied science. Engineers are the people who make the applications. They are by nature not dreamers but doers—builders, tinkerers, realists. Typically they are people who showed a fascination with gadgetry from an early age, who pulled radios apart and put them back together while other kids were shooting marbles. When they get to engineering school, they are taught to think rationally and to express

themselves in mathematical terms. They learn to reason analytically, to pull a problem apart and to examine it logically and resolve it with precision. They learn that there is a single right answer to every question. They learn about elegance and simplicity, but not about subtlety or ambiguity.

Post industrial society requires more than just a lot of engineers. It requires engineers with the vision and the foresight to see where they are going and the verbal capacity to tell us about it. The real problem with engineering students is not that they're driven by the desire to make twenty-five thousand dollars a year—that's just their way of putting the quest for self-fulfillment in quantifiable terms. The problem with engineering students is the problem with everybody else in America: they can't seem to bridge the two sides of knowledge [, the sciences and the humanities]. Our institutions, in other words, are not developing the integrative functions required for the thoughtful application of complex systems.[8]

THE PROBLEMS OF LIFE
ARE NOT LIKE RUBIK'S CUBE

In a phrase, *we have bred a nation of certainty-junkies.* We have trained the members of our culture to expect a daily dosage of highly structured-bounded exercises. The difficulty is that the problems of organizations and society have become highly *unstructured* and *unbounded.*

It is no accident that Rubik's Cube has become as popular as it has in our culture. Rubik's Cube is the epitome of a bounded-structured exercise. It appeals to the structured side of our personality, or what brain physiologists metaphorically refer to as left-hemispherical thinking, i.e., the side of our brain which prefers logical reasoning, which processes information linearly, thinks analytically, quantitatively, etc.

Rubik's Cube is a bounded exercise in the sense that there is a definite limit to the absolute number of ways in which one can arrange the colored faces of the cube. True, this number is in the millions but it is a definite number that can be computed and hence known. Thus, the number of the ways in which the faces of the cube can be arranged is bounded. The exercise is also highly structured in that one can specify a definite procedure which if it is followed will guarantee a correct solution to the puzzle; all the separate facets on each face will have the same color and each face as a whole will have a different color from all the other faces.

In defense of Rubik's Cube, it is at least fun. Unlike most exercises, it is at least aesthetic. It's both pretty and cerebral at the same time. Further, it's not merely a head-exercise but a hand one as well. It appeals more than most puzzles do to both the left and the right sides of our brains simultaneously.

It's vital that as a culture we come to appreciate that there is a vast and important difference between structured-bounded exercises and unstructured-unbounded problems. True problems are unbounded because unlike Rubik's Cube there is rarely if ever a single way to define "the problem," let alone a single solution as to what is to count as an answer.

It is more vital than ever to appreciate that the type of education needed to solve exercises is radically different from that which is needed to cope with problems. The unthinkable is not an exercise; it is a member of the class of wicked problems. Education for the unthinkable is education for handling vast amounts of uncertainty, for handling fundamental differences in the ways that different stakeholders perceive a problem, and for helping them to turn their differences into a positive asset. In effect, no single stakeholder has the definitive formulation of a problem. Conversely, each picks up an aspect of the problem that the others may neglect. Coping with corporate tragedies thus consists of learning how to seek out radically different perceptions of important issues in the first place and in learning how to integrate them productively in the second place. If the reader can bear with us, then later chapters will show how to do this.

UNSTRUCTURING THE LEFT BRAIN, STRUCTURING THE RIGHT

Unfortunately, the vast if not overwhelming majority of courses and books in university courses, certainly in the sciences and professions, consist of endless amounts of structured exercises. A truly rare exception is a delightful book by two distinguished social scientists, Charles A. Lave and James G. March, *An Introduction to Models in the Social Sciences.*[9] Lave and March's book is chock full of problems, not exercises. Indeed, there is not a single exercise in it. That is, every situation which is presented to the student has more than one right way to define the problem underlying the presenting situation or initiating symptom, and as a result, has more than one correct answer.

The book is a virtual primer on the different kind of thinking that a complex society requires. It unabashedly instructs students into the joy, the fun, and even the beauty of formulating problems from radically different viewpoints. A typical example that we have used with continued success with MBA students and corporate executives is the following:

A few years ago, Detroit had a six-month newspaper strike that closed down all its newspapers. During the strike, Detroit's suicide rate fell very sharply (that is, there were far fewer suicides), but returned to its usual rate when the papers resumed publishing. (This is true, by the way).[10]

In relation to this problem the student is instructed to:

(a) Make up two *abstract* models that would account for the observation [in this case, the falling suicide rate during the strike].
(b) Generate a *total* of three interesting predictions from the two models and identify which model each prediction is derived from.
(c) Find some critical fact/situation/observation/prediction that will distinguish between the two models. It should be *observable* and you should make it clear how you would observe it [i.e., either the fact, situation, observation, or prediction].[11]

In the years that we have used this problem, it has never failed to stir both controversy and interest. Indeed, the two may be inseparable.

We have also added a wrinkle that makes it of special interest to practitioners and students of business. After they have responded to the problem initially as it is stated, we have asked them to find a situation in the business world that is analogous to it. Our respondents have had no trouble in finding parallels, e.g., the effects of company and industry newsletters on the premature death of new products, businesses, etc. In short, we have found that the minds of managers can be stretched to the demands of today's world *if* they are presented with materials that challenge them and wean them away from the debilitating effects of their prior training, i.e., a steady diet of puzzles and exercises.

It must of course be noted that it is undoubtedly more difficult to undo that which shouldn't have been done in the first place. One of the major problems connected with adult learning is that of first *unlearning* that which shouldn't have been learned in the first place. There is some promising research which shows that contrary to conventional wisdom, children can be taught to handle uncertainty and in general to think differently. Psychologist Joan Sieber and her colleagues bluntly state:

There is evidence that students seldom are taught appropriate ways of dealing with uncertainty. On the contrary, they usually are taught to regard problems as having clear and determinate solutions and to look to others for the answers. [Researchers have observed] that teachers usually provide students with specific information and then expect specific "right" answers to questions about that information. Children hunt for cues to what answer the teacher expects. Furthermore, it appears that teachers do not often allow questioning interruptions from students. The results of this regimen is as one might expect: when questioned about problematic matters, students usually give simple, dogmatic answers. . . .

In response to this problem, a program of research on warranted uncertainty was initiated, and instructional materials were designed to teach children to identify questions that warrant uncertainty and to analyze such questions to determine *why* uncertainty is warranted. Sieber [and her colleagues] identified five types of questions and developed a simple procedure for teaching students to distinguish among them. The five types of questions are as follows:

(1) Questions that do not warrant uncertainty; questions to which the individual knows the answer. In most cases, the following questions fall into this category: What is your name? What state do you live in? What is your birthdate?

(2) Questions to which the individual does not know the right answer but to which the answer is known by someone or is available from some other already existing source. For most people, the following questions would fall into this category: Who invented the sewing machine? What principles underlie jet propulsion?

(3) Questions to which no one may know the answer but for which there is a known method of discovering the answer. Many carefully formulated empirical questions fall into this category, for instance: What is the volume of this room? What is my blood sugar level at present?

(4) Questions to which no one knows the answer for sure because the questions concern events that have not yet happened, such as: When will there be another earthquake that measures 7 or higher on the Richter scale? When will ice again cover all of Canada?

(5) Questions to which no one knows the answer and for which there is at present no known way to discover the answer, such as: Is there life in other galaxies? What are the smallest physical components of matter?[12]

Sieber and her colleagues showed that not only could students be trained to differentiate between these fundamentally different kinds of questions but that as a result they were more tolerant of uncertainty, and as a result, able to handle it more productively. Further, the effects were lasting long after the training had occurred. Most telling of all, those who had been through the training were more resistant than those who had not to peer pressure with regard to taking drugs! Apparently the training had helped the students to be more skeptical regarding the touted but unsupported benefits of drugs.

Reeducating kids is one thing, but reeducating MBAs and practicing managers is another. And yet even on this front there are some signs that something different is in the air. For one thing, both practitioners and business school educators are openly airing in the national media their dissatisfaction with current management education.[13]

One of the clearest ways to identify what's currently wrong in a society is to locate the objects of its jokes. For instance, McNeil surely had to know that its brand name Tylenol was in deep trouble when it became the object of sick jokes. When the very name of a product becomes identified with trouble, it can spell the kiss of death to a manufacturer.

While MBA education is far from such a condition, there are signs that it has entered its joke phase. For instance, Professor William Hamilton, director of the management and technology program at the prestigious Wharton School at the University of Pennsylvania, is reputed by *Business Week* to have said in response to the charge that business schools "are still largely geared to turning out number-crunchers. 'One of the solutions to the Japanese threat is to export a number of our MBA programs to Japan.'"[14]

For another sign, a growing number of major corporations have either turned to starting up their own in-house schools for educating managers or they are beefing up what they've had already. True, some of these programs such as McDonald's famous Hamburger U imbue their personnel with "the company philosophy" or "the culture" of the organization. However, others such as GE are attempting to educate their employees how to think, and not to plug numbers mindlessly into formulas that, no matter how good they may be, are no substitute for serious thinking.[15]

Still another promising sign is the recent establishment of an electronic university, the School of Management and Strategic Studies (SMSS) at the Western Behavioral Sciences Institute in La Jolla, California. The computer plays a central role in SMSS in that instead of being locked into a rigid schedule that proves to be the undoing of most executive programs, busy executives can "telecommute" to the school at their convenience. They do not physically have to be at SMSS in order to benefit from it. There are some advantages to being part of an extended computer network.

However vital the computer is, it is not the heart of the curriculum at SMSS. As a recent article in *Fortune* described it:

> There is...a deep philosophic difference [between SMSS's curriculum and that of most business schools]. The [SMSS] offers no quantitative courses. It ignores the [Harvard Business School] case-study approach widely used in other programs, as well as their conventional subject matter—finance, marketing, and the usual craft of management. It concentrates instead on the humanities and social sciences...the school's main objective is to develop a "long view" so that executives will "emerge

from the two-year program with an ability to balance short-term profitability against long-term viability."

Dick Farson [the founder of SMSS] contends that corporate leaders face too much complexity and turbulence to rely on old quantitative solutions. "They must look at things as interconnected systems rather than in terms of cause and effect," he says. To provide the long view, Farson has signed on professors with diverse specialties: philosophers, anthropologists, futurists, even a climatologist—lofty thinkers who don't always relate to the bottom line problems of business. But then these are the folks ("flakes," some executives say when they first enter the program) Farson has been surrounded by throughout his career.[16]

CONCLUDING COMMENTS

Education today is part of the profound crisis in which the world finds itself. The crisis of education is due to the fact that we are teaching students to apply outmoded concepts to problems for which they are no longer adequate. These concepts only worsen things, not make them better:

> We find ourselves today in a state of profound, worldwide crisis. We can read about the various aspects of this crisis every day in the newspapers. We have an energy crisis, a health-care crisis, high inflation and unemployment, pollution and other environmental disasters, the ever-increasing threat of nuclear war, a rising wave of violence and crime, and so on.
>
> All of these threats are actually different facets of one and the same crisis—essentially a crisis of perception. We are trying to apply the concepts of an outdated world view—the mechanistic world view of Cartesian-Newtonian science—to a reality that can no longer be understood in these terms.
>
> We live in a globally interconnected world, in which biological, psychological, social, and environmental phenomena are all interdependent. To describe this world appropriately we need an ecological perspective that the Cartesian world view cannot offer.
>
> What we need, then, is a fundamental change in our thoughts, perceptions, and values. The beginnings of this change are already visible in all fields, and the shift from a mechanistic to a holistic conception of reality is likely to dominate the entire decade. The gravity and global extent of our crisis indicate that the current changes are likely to result in a transformation of unprecedented dimensions, a turning point for the planet as a whole.[17]

NOTES

1. "A Conversation With Peter Drucker," *Psychology Today*, December 1982, p. 62.

2. Robert Reich, *The Next American Frontier* (New York: New York Times Book Co., 1983), p. 215.

3. William V. Muse, "If All the Business Schools in the Country Were Eliminated...Would Anyone Notice?" *Collegiate News and Views* 36 (Spring 1983):1–5.

4. Robert A. Gordon and James E. Howell, *Higher Education for Business* (New York: Columbia University Press, 1959); Frank C. Pierson, *The Education of American Businessmen* (New York: McGraw Hill, 1959).

5. Muse, *If All the Business Schools*, p. 3.

6. Lester C. Thurow, *Dangerous Currents, The State of Economics* (New York: Random House 1983), pp. xviii–xix.

7. Dennis A. Williams, et al., "Can the Schools Be Saved?" *Newsweek*, May 9, 1983, pp. 50–58.

8. Frank Rose, "The Mass Production of Engineers," *Esquire*, May 1983, pp. 76, 84.

9. Charles A. Lave and James G. March, *An Introduction to Models in the Social Sciences* (New York: Harper and Row 1975).

10. Ibid., p. 83.

11. Ibid.

12. Joan E. Sieber, Richard E. Clark, Helen H. Smith, and Nancy Sanders, "Warranted Uncertainty and Students' Knowledge and Use of Drugs," *Contemporary Educational Psychology* 3 (1978):31.

13. "A New Era for Management," *Business Week*, April 25, 1983, pp. 50–84.

14. Ibid., p. 80.

15. Ibid.

16. Roy Rowan, "Executive Ed. At Computer U.," *Fortune*, March 7, 1983, p. 59.

17. Fritjof Capra, "The Turning Point: A New Vision of Reality," *The Futurist*, December 1982, p. 19.

4

The Loneliness of the Psychopath:
What Business Schools Fail to Teach About Human Behavior Can Be Deadly to Your Organization

Can we say that society currently reinforces sociopathic behavior?...the evidence would seen to indicate that we do provide a surprising amount of intermittent reinforcement. One can well speculate that we have come out of the age of anxiety and into an age of sociopathy.[1]

D.A. Rockwell

What is different about our culture today is not that Americans have new *desires.* The same desires persist from one generation to the next. But now the culture endorses as morally acceptable many desires that were not acceptable in the past. . . . Today few. . .actions are unthinkable, or un-thought, or unacted upon.[2]

D. Yankelovich

Of all the aspects connected with corporate tragedies none are as fascinating and as frustrating as those which pertain to the kinds of individuals who engage in such acts. Nothing becomes more apparent than in dealing effectively with the kinds of individuals who are more likely to create tragedies, one needs a concept of human behavior that goes far beyond that which is discussed in the typical business school curriculum.

As we made clear in Chapters 2 and 3, the curricula of most business schools and the thinking of most managers are a direct holdover from the industrial revolution. In that view of the world, a complex and sophisticated concept of man was rendered unnecessary, if not precluded altogether, by the image of the world as a simple machine. The human psyche was literally conceived of as a simple, impersonal, objective calculating machine.

Especially in this century, it has become painfully obvious that human beings do not behave like this at all. As Freud and Jung repeatedly showed us, human behavior is influenced by forces and instincts of which most people are unconscious. To the long list of mankind's great illusions (e.g., perfect love, the perfect marriage, the perfect car, perfectly behaved children, a truly wise and loving country, etc.) must be added the illusion of an unbiased, totally conscious, objective human mind. No matter what the field of human endeavor, there is no such thing as a human actor who is able to know the full set of actions that ought to be considered and how to assign the benefits versus the costs associated with those actions independently of a complex set of human desires, passions, and wants.[3]

This chapter shows that we can gain considerable insight into the minds of those individuals who are more likely to engage in unthinkable acts. Modern psychoanalytic theories have advanced to where they can shed considerable light on the innermost workings of the human mind.

It is not the purpose of this chapter to discuss the full range of the different kinds of personalities that could be associated with every one of the corporate tragedies that we presented in Chapter 1. Such a task is beyond the scope of this book. For each tragedy, there are a number of different kinds of personality constellations that could be associated with each of them, not one. Our task is to show that as complex as the human mind is it is not impossibly or inordinately complex such as to defy all explanation. This chapter constitutes a glimpse into the nature of this complexity.

In discussing matters as intricate and emotionally laden as the unthinkable, we suffer from what we call the "zero-infinity mentality or complex": "If we can't have perfect or complete knowledge (i.e., infinite social knowledge) about all those who commit such acts and exactly where they can be located before they commit them, then we can't have any knowledge about them at all." Thus, we either have infinite or zero social knowledge. We would suggest that between perfect and complete knowledge (infinity) and no knowledge (zero), there is a lot of room for discussion and for learning. Such strict dichotomies (zero and infinity) are characteristic of rigid either/or type thinking. As such, they are only applicable to the world when conceived as a simple machine. Either one had perfect and complete knowledge about every part of the machine or one had no knowledge at all. Such rigid either/or's are no longer helpful in coping with today's complex world.

To make our task both more manageable and at the same time more accessible to a larger lay audience, we shall restrict our discussion to two main types of disruptive personalities. The first is a discussion of the *inner psychodynamics* of the psychopathic personality.[4] The second is a discussion of the *outer behavioral* characteristics of those individuals who are prone to engage in bizarre crimes or in acts of terrorism.[5] As we shall see, there are considerable overlaps between these two types. Thus, a discussion of the one helps in understanding the other.

STAKEHOLDERS OF THE HUMAN MIND

One of the most incredible findings of psychoanalysis was the discovery that the workings of the human psyche could be understood in terms of the interactions between a constellation of inner selves. If the nature of a modern corporation can only be understood in terms of the multitude of stakeholders, both internal and external to it, with which it engages, then in principle the same applies to the human psyche.[6] The human psyche can also be viewed as composed of a multitude of inner stakeholders that are no less fascinating and complex than those which compose the external social entity known as the corporation. A major difference, however, is that we need a slightly more complex diagram to indicate the structure of the human psyche than the diagrams which sufficed in Chapter 2 to indicate the structure of the corporation.

Figure 4-1 is a gross simplification of the structure of the adult human psyche.[7] (In this illustration, the mother.) It uses the metaphor of a boat or ship to show that most if not the vast majority of the structure of the human psyche lies beneath the plane of consciousness. The ego or that part of the human psyche that is tuned to dealing with internal and external reality, i.e., consciousness, constitutes only a small part of the totality of the human mind. Most of the contents of the human mind lie below the plane of human consciousness. They are not easily or readily available for inspection by the person in whom they reside.

Paradoxically, even only a part of the ego itself, that part of the psyche whose function it is to deal with conscious reality, lies above the plane of the unconscious. Significant parts of the ego are forever rooted

FIGURE 4-1

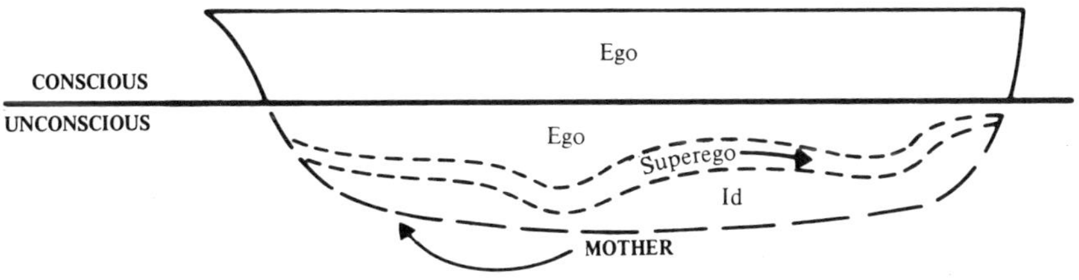

The Structure of the Adult Psyche

in the unconscious parts of the mind because it is only out of the unconscious that the ego originally arose and developed.

The deepest layers of the mind are termed the id. The id constitutes the original sources of life energies, biological instincts, instinctual energies, primitive drives, archaic forces, etc., that form and propel the human animal. The id in short constitutes the primitive and original reservoir of instinctual energy that makes up the core of human beings.

In terms of this relatively simple diagram, the superego may be thought of as a kind of buffer or a baffle between the ego and the id, although it must be strongly emphasized that in no way are we dealing with either rigid entities or rigid boundaries between them. The entities which constitute the psyche are not only in a state of constant evolution but in one of dynamic tension and fluid motion between them as well.

The superego acts as a kind of dynamic regulator or a baffle between the primitive and often uncontrollable instincts, wishes, desires of the id and the conscious reality functioning aspects of the ego. As such, the superego is in constant danger of being overwhelmed by the potent forces and energies of the id whose function it is to contain. If the superego is overwhelmed, then we speak of the ego as being invaded by the tremendous forces of the id. In some cases the invasion is so powerful and so complete that we speak of the breakup and dissolution of the ego. The weakened or greatly threatened ego literally sinks back down below the plane of consciousness. We then speak of a break with or a loss of contact with reality.

Figure 4–2 shows how the psyche of the child develops in relationship to the primary stakeholder in his life, the mother. Because of his initial helplessness and prolonged dependency on others to satisfy his basic needs, the newborn human infant is for all practical purposes in an initial state of total unconsciousness or total symbiotic union with the mother just as before birth. Although by being born he is now outside of the womb, his dependency on the parents is so great that he is still in a state of near total fusion with the parents, but above all, especially with the mother. In the beginning, the child *is* nothing but an extension of the mother.

The dotted little "boat" on the left within the larger "vessel"[8] of the mother is meant to indicate that in the beginning the psyche of the child is contained entirely within the psyche of the mother. Notice carefully that the plane of consciousness of the child is *not* the same as the plane of consciousness of the mother. The consciousness of the child is initially defined in relation to the psyche of the mother. What's conscious for the mother is still unconscious for the child. Another way to put this is to say that in the beginning, the ego of the mother (or more broadly the parents) substitutes for the nonexistent, undeveloped ego of the infant. The

FIGURE 4-2

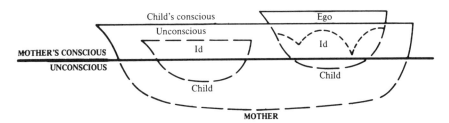

The Structure of the Infant Psyche

child has yet to separate himself from the psyche of the mother so that his ego (as the small boat on the right shows) can rise above the plane of its unconsciousness, the mother. In the beginning, all is id. Ego has yet to develop, to make its appearance.

This is not the place to enter into a long and detailed discussion of Freudian psychology, particularly the developmental aspects of the psyche, but one aspect in particular does need emphasizing. Because of the critical dependency of the child on the mother, because of his initial strong fusion with and hence lack of separate identity, from the child's perspective in the beginning the mother is as much an extension of the child as the child is an extension of the mother. As a result of this prolonged fusion with the mother, the child identifies so strongly with the body of the mother, the initial source of his vital nourishment, that the child forms a mental image of the mother within his own developing psyche. He develops his mind by forming a mental image of the first object outside of him, his mother.

The child identifies unconsciously so strongly with the body and the personality of the mother that he introjects or takes into his own developing mental apparatus parts of the mother's and the father's psyches. The child's personality develops out of the unconscious modeling of the parents' personalities.

In other words, the internal stakeholders which compose the personality system of the child are formed from the internal stakeholders which compose the personality systems of the parents. The formation of the human personality is one of the most dramatic examples of the powerful influence of one stakeholder system on that of another.

Thus far, all this is of course the version of the psyche according to Freud. What Jung did was to show, much like modern nuclear physicists, that each of the subparts of Freud's model of the mind (id, ego, superego) was in turn composed of innumerable other parts. There are in short a host of innumerable solar systems within solar systems. These other parts Jung termed "archetypes." Archetypes may be thought of as those aspects of the mind which embody man's deepest felt concerns with symbols. For instance, typical examples of archetypes are religious symbols of all kinds: the lamb and the fish which stand for Christ; the cross; the circle symbolizing wholeness, containment, etc.

This aspect of man's mind shall concern us in Chapter 7 for it has to do with one of the more bizarre aspects of the unthinkable that we discussed in Chapter 1. This feature has to do with the cases of projection, e.g., those individuals who saw evil in the logo of Procter and Gamble. In cases of this kind, one typically projects aspects of one's own internal psyche that one does not like out onto the external world. Since projection operates unconsciously, one is usually totally unaware that the external thing to which one is reacting so strongly is in reality an aspect of one's inner self that one does not like. It's easier to blame something external for one's shortcomings than oneself. We encountered a classic example of this in the business world in Chapter 1 where Monolithic Motors chose to blame an external stakeholder, the government, for its woes rather than to accept that it, M.M., might be responsible for many of its faults.

With this background, we are ready to turn to the loneliness of the psychopath.

A BRIEF JOURNEY INTO
THE WORLD OF THE PSYCHOPATH

In a field as complex as human behavior and where as a result there are so many controversies regarding the appropriate way to study it, it is therefore all the more surprising to find that there is a rather remarkable degree of agreement as to identifying characteristics of the psychopath.[9] Elliott's description is as succinct and to the point as any:

> Since [Prichard in 1835 proposed one of the first descriptions]...the list of symptons has been expanded to include inadequately motivated [social] behavior, aggression, absence of conscience (and therefore absence of neurotic anxiety), inability to distinguish between truth and falsehood or between fact and fantasy, lack of insight, lack of judgment when faced with alternative courses of action, failure to learn from...experience (including punishment), imperception, lack of natural affection, impersonal response to sexual partners, absence of a normal sense of fear, capacity for ingratiation, impulsiveness, total egocentricity with constant disregard for other people's feelings and interests, inability to foresee or worry about the results of their actions, and proneness to pathological intoxi-

cation with alcohol. In consequence their lives reveal "a persistent pattern of self defeat."[10]

It is vitally important to stress as Elliott and virtually everyone in the field does that each item in the list above must be thought of as part of a complex mosaic. While they tend to go together as a whole, every single item is not necessarily present in every case of psychopathy. Further, every investigator does not necessarily give the same interpretation or weight to every item. Still, as an overall pattern, the list conveys a good portrait of the psychopath.

Time and again, a critical factor that emerges from the case studies of psychopaths is that as children, in the critical early years in the formation of their personalities, they did not receive the crucial physical and emotional nourishment from their parents that would allow them to form a healthy self-concept of themselves, of others, and of themselves in relation to others. The parents of psychopaths, the critical role models that as children psychopaths had available for identification, i.e., the stakeholders that psychopaths had available for introjection and thus for formation of the deepest core of their personality, were themselves deficient. The childhood histories of psychopaths show a marked and repeated pattern of "massive deprivation," of parental abuse in one form or another. They were not, in the emotional sense, properly fed by their parents. In Freudian terms, they were not properly cared for during the critical preoedipal, oral stage of their development. As Leaff has put it:

[The delinquent's] disregard for the rights of others and lack of consideration for their feelings could result only if his earliest experiences at the hands of others were similarly characterized without much regard for, or consideration of, *his own* needs, feelings, and welfare.[11]

Further:

When oedipal and preoedipal attitudes and experiences are too depriving or violent, and remain unresolved, the child is not able to make the necessary differentiation between important individuals in the family constellation and those in the environment. The environment becomes an extended battleground for the acting out of such unresolved conflicts. For example, aggressive and destructive images of the oral phase, sadomasochistic fantasies of the anal phase, exhibitionistic fantasies, castration fears and family romance with feelings of being isolated and unloved are transferred to the external world where they become a hindrance to social adjustment.[12]

In sum, the psychopath is the dual and lifelong prisoner of those who improperly cared for him in life's first beginnings. On the one hand, he wants to strike back with a fury and a rage that is born from one of the cruelest experiences that ever could befall any human being, emotional mistreatment and/or abandonment by those that one had no initial choice over whatsoever in selecting to satisfy one's basic needs. In effect, *the psychopath spends the rest of his life getting back at his parents through society.* Indeed, since one's parents initially *are* society, and since the parents are bad, and further since bad role models do not help the child to make valid differentiations between himself and the environment, the child perpetually strikes back at all the objects in his environment in a totally undifferentiated manner; i.e., everything outside him is bad.

At the same time, and perhaps even crueler, the role models that the child has available for the development of his personality, whether good or bad, are the only ones he has available. From what we understand of the development of personality, the child has to have something available to introject if he is to develop a personality. Thus, by virtue of prolonged contact with his parents, whether good or bad, he takes into his own personality the very outer objects he despises. *He thus carries around a lifelong rage toward his parents but also toward the deepest inner parts of himself.* The only ways in which he knows how to handle those parts of himself he despises is to project them out onto others and then to attack them aggressively. More socially desirable ways of handling his frustration and anger are closed off to him by the very conditions which set the whole process in motion. His parents themselves generally lacked the very mechanisms for handling frustration that could have provided a basis for the child's doing so. The child thus perpetuates and keeps alive for yet another generation a social disease that is as potent as anything that could be biologically transmitted. Furthermore, while in our society individuals are and should be held responsible for their "own" behavior, it is difficult to hold the child solely responsible for stopping or undoing, especially without significant help from others, that which his own parents as "adults" were unable to stop in their own lives.

If Freud succeeded to any extent at all in giving us a glimpse, however tenuous and obscured it was, into the deepest recesses of the human soul, then we believe he showed that the earliest and therefore one of the most critical phases of human development was what he labeled the "oral phase." The oral phase is literally what its name implies, the stage of human development where one takes in without giving back. Is it really so hard to understand that if one was not properly nourished in the beginning of one's life that one would spend the rest of one's life trying to obtain that which one should have received initially? Further, is it thereby so hard to understand that if one's initial oral deprivation was so great that one would naturally want to deprive others of their oral satisfaction?

Now we are finally ready to make the leap. If all of the above is true or at the very least plausible, and further, if modern society provides an abundance of opportunities for the psychopath not just to strike out randomly but to strike out deliberately, to try to soothe the core of his hurt, his oral deprivation, then what better way to express this than through the literal spoiling of the oral intake of others? In a society that not only provides seemingly endless opportunities for disruption but also one that increasingly has lost the quality of community, what could be more characteristic of the psychopath than to pick the media of food and medicine to stage his outbreaks of personal pain and anger toward society?

THE MORE BIZARRE THE CRIME, THE STRONGER THE PROFILE

Thus far, one of the main contentions of this chapter has been that as complex as human behavior is, it is not so complex as to defy all description or understanding. Indeed, if human behavior defied all description or understanding then there could be no such thing as human communication, let alone of the written variety that we are engaging in now, since all communication presupposes some widely accepted and shared set of generic categories for pigeonholing experience.

This does not mean that we currently know, or that we ever will, all the diverse reasons men have buried deep within them that motivate their behavior. Neither does it mean, thank God, that we will ever be able to predict fully what people will do in all kinds of situations. As we stressed earlier, it is *not* a strict either/or; i.e., either we know everything there is to know about human behavior or we thereby know nothing. Strict either/or's are not the appropriate way to think about things that are as complex as human beings.

Paradoxically, whether it is in attempting to understand what goes on deepest inside of man or in attempting to understand what goes on outside of him without any reference whatsoever to his deepest impulses, it is easier to start with the most extreme or bizarre cases of human behavior first. Was it not Freud after all who showed that an understanding of abnormal behavior provided a window into the understanding of so-called normal behavior, that so-called neurotics were merely all of us writ a bit more extreme and larger?

Increasingly, police units around the country have turned to a technique known as psychological profiling to help them in stalking criminals. Provided by the FBI, the technique is especially helpful in giving police units a portrait of the kinds of criminals involved in especially gruesome or bizarre crimes. Indeed, the more gruesome or bizarre the crime the easier it is to paint a portrait of the criminal involved. It takes no genius to figure out that such persons are generally suffering from major psychological abnormalities and hence ought to be more easily differentiated from the mass of people who generally speaking are only suffering from the universal abnormality called "normalcy."

There is another and much more disturbing reason for concentrating on the extreme or bizarre. In recent years, bizarre crimes have increased significantly. According the the FBI, 20 years ago the rule of thumb was "that in more than 80 percent of murder cases, the killer had some kind of previous relationship with the victim. The motive was passionate anger or a desire for revenge, and a quick canvas of the neighborhood usually turned up a list of likely suspects."[13]

In recent times, this 80 percent figure has dropped sharply. "Out of the 22,516 killings in the country in 1981, some *45 percent* [emphasis ours] were either 'stranger murders,' in which killer and victim had never seen each other before the crime, or murders in which the killer was listed as 'unknown.'. . .in an increasingly large number of 'stranger' homicides, the killer seems driven to murder not by some 'rational' reason or easily understood emotion, but by a serious psychological disorder. The FBI estimates that as many as 75 percent of killings may now fall into this category."[14]

It is not our purpose to enter into a detailed discussion of the various kinds of criminal profiles that emerge. In many ways, the profiles parallel the discussion in the previous section. This is all the more significant in that the FBI tends to avoid, if not disavow, "deep psychological insight than [to rely] on statistical probabilities, plain common sense, and the experience gained from looking at hundreds of similar cases."[15]

For the purposes of our discussion, the fact that human behavior can be profiled at all is the important thing. The fact that even the most offensive, outrageous, and bizarre behavior can be patterned shows that underneath it all there is a kind of order, however strange, to the human condition. Thus for our purposes it is important to see that there is a method to the FBI's manner of studying madness.

Profilers pay particular attention to the manner in which a person was killed, the kind of weapon that was used, something the bureau calls "post-offense behavior," or what the killer did to the victim after he or she was dead. Sex murders typically are stabbings, strangulations, or beatings, rather than shootings. If the killer brought along his own weapon, it points to a stabber, someone fairly well organized, even cunning, who came from another part of town and probably drove a car. If the killer used whatever was available—a knife from the kitchen or a lamp cord—it points to a more impulsive, a more disorganized personality. It also means that the person probably came on foot and lives nearby.

Was there a lot of beating about the face? The general rule is that a brutal facial attack. . .means that the killer knew the victim; the more brutal the attack, the closer the relationship. Was the victim killed immediately in a blitz style of assault? This usually indicates a younger killer, someone in his teens or early 20s, who feels threatened by his victims and needs to render them harmless right away. On the other hand, if the killer showed mastery of the situation, if he killed slowly and methodically, it points to a more sadistic personality, a man in his late 20s or 30s.''[16]

CONCLUDING REMARKS

We have made considerable progress in recognizing, diagnosing, and even treating severe forms of antisocial human behavior. Why people really do what they do will always remain an enigma in part, perhaps in large part. But we need not feel either totally overwhelmed or powerless in our understanding, if not in our ability to control, such behavior. For instance, interesting progress has been made on such fronts as constructing computer programs that can successfully differentiate between real and false suicide notes or true and false terrorist threats.[17] We now have a much better understanding of the kinds of individuals who engage in terrorism. For instance, Miron,[18] one of the investigators who has studied the phenomenon extensively, feels that "many terrorist acts are really 'passive-aggressive' attempts at suicide, creating situations in which the police are forced to attack [the terrorists.]."[19]

We also have a better understanding of the behavior of those who are taken hostage. For instance, early on in the study of terrorist activities, the so-called Stockholm Effect was discovered. This occurred during a hostage incident, in Stockholm appropriately enough, wherein one of the female hostages fell in love with one of the hostage-takers. As strange as this phenomenon is, it is understandable, if only in principle, if we go back to our earlier discussion in this chapter of the psychological mechanisms of identification and introjection. As will be recalled, the mechanisms of identification and introjection are two of the most powerful means by which human beings form their personality. As such, they remain in operation throughout all of one's life. They do not cease to operate once one has attained adulthood. They are such powerful mechanisms that they can sometimes even cause us to link up with our natural enemies. Again, all of this is really not so strange if we simply perceive that in hostage situations, the hostage is usually dependent on the hostage-taker for life and death, food and sustenance, over an extended period of time. Is it therefore really any surprise to find that people would revert back to primitive emotions and basic modes of childhood dependency in such cases?[20]

This is also not the place to enter into a prolonged discussion of the fact that there exist detailed guides concerning how to negotiate with hostage-takers.[21] Suffice it to say that they not only exist but they provide detailed helpful how-to guides in negotiating with hostage-takers of different psychological profiles. Further, the profiles of those individuals who are best equipped to deal with terrorists or hostage-takers are also well known by now. We thus know how to identify and to train those individuals best-suited from a psychological standpoint to negotiate with hostage-takers.

Has it not become clear that we have been calling for the emergence of a new and very different kind of scientific discipline and profession: industrial psychiatry? Of necessity we have only been able to scratch the surface of the kinds of personalities that are prepared to wage battle against the goods, products, services and personnel of the modern corporation. But even from this brief accounting, is it still not clear that the modern corporation could benefit greatly from the services of industrial psychiatry? Most of all, is it not clear that the modern corporation ultimately has no choice but to take deadly seriously the task of asking itself, "What are the various kinds of extreme antisocial stakeholders who exist, and what are the various ways that our corporation is vulnerable to them?" Not to ask these questions in today's world, not even to consider them, is one of the surest forms of institutional suicide. In a word, the modern corporation must learn to think like a psychopath if it is to guard itself from the actions of psychopaths.

Knowing thy mind and that of thine enemies are no longer abstract philosophical dictums. They are necessities in today's world. As the world has grown in complexity, our concepts of the minds that inhabit it must change and grow accordingly. Simpleminded concepts of mind are no longer adequate.

NOTES

1. Don A. Rockwell, "Social and Familial Correlates of Antisocial Disorders," in *The Psychopath, A Comprehensive Study of Antisocial Disorders and Behaviors,* ed. William H. Reid (New York: Bruner/Mazel 1978), p. 140.

2. Daniel Yankelovich, *New Rules, Searching for Self-Fulfillment in a World Turned Upside Down* (New York: Bantam, 1981), p. 241.

3. For instance, in the field of physical science, the reader is referred to an earlier study that shows the tremendous biases, emotions, and passions that enter into the doing of science. See Ian I. Mitroff, *The Subjective Side of Science, A Philosophical Inquiry into the Psychology of the Apollo Moon Scientists* (Amsterdam: Elsevier, 1974). Forty-two of the most prestigious scientists, including two Nobel Prize winners, who studied the moon rocks returned by the Apollo missions freely admitted the tremendous and at times positive role that strong biases, emotions, and passions played in the conduct of science. Good scientists are no less

passionate, maybe even more so, than anyone else in defending their ideas against all attacks.

4. For an extensive treatment, see Louis A. Leaff, "The Antisocial Personalilty: Psychodynamic Implications," *The Psychopath, A Comprehensive Study of Antisocial Disorders and Behaviors*, ed. William H. Reid (New York: Bruner/Mazel, 1978) pp. 79–117; for general background, see the classic by Otto Fenichel, *The Psychoanalytic Theory of Neurosis* (New York: W.W. Norton, 1972).

5. See Murray S. Miron and Arnold P. Goldstein, *Hostage* (New York: Pergamon, 1979); see also Yonah Alexander, David Carlton, and Paul Wilkinson, eds., *Terrorism: Theory and Practice* (Boulder Col.: Westview, 1979); Christopher Dobson and Ronald Payne, *The Terrorists: Their Weapons, Leaders, and Tactics* (New York: Facts on File, 1982).

6. See Ian I. Mitroff, *Stakeholders of the Organizational Mind, The Nature and Function of Archetypes in Social and Organizational Life* (San Francisco: Jossey-Bass, 1983).

7. For more complex diagrams but which in principle are the same, see Daniel Lawrence O'Keefe, *Stolen Lightning, The Social Theory of Magic* (New York: Continuum, 1982), pp. 280, 287–89, 291, 293, 295.

8. The metaphor of a "vessel" or a "container" is one of the primary, worldwide archetypal images of the female. See Erich Neumann, *The Great Mother, An Analysis of the Archetype* (Princeton, N.J.: Princeton University Press, Bollingen Series XLVII, 1974).

9. For an overview of various views, see Robert D. Hare, *Psychopathy: Theory and Research* (New York: John Wiley, 1970); Charles F. Reed, Irving E. Alexander, and Silvan S. Tomkins, eds., *Psychopathology, A Source Book* (Cambridge, Mass.: Harvard University Press, 1963); and William H. Reid, ed., *The Psychopath, A Comprehensive Study of Antisocial Disorders and Behaviors* (New York: Bruner/Mazel, 1978).

10. Frank A. Elliott, "Neurological Aspects of Antisocial Behavior," in *The Psychopath, A Comprehensive Study of Antisocial Disorders and Behaviors*, ed. William H. Reid (New York: Bruner/Mazel, 1978), p. 147.

11. Leaff, "The Antisocial Personality," pp. 85–86.

12. Ibid., p. 87.

13. Bruce Porter, "Mind Hunters, Tracking Down Killers With the FBI's Psychological Profiling Team," *Psychology Today*, April 1983, pp. 42–48.

14. Ibid.

15. Ibid., p. 48.

16. Ibid., pp. 47–48.

17. Berkeley Rice, "Between the Lines of Threatening Messages," *Psychology Today*, September 1981, pp. 52–64.

18. See Miron and Goldstein, *Hostage*.

19. Rice, "Between the Lines of Threatening Messages," p. 64.

20. See Miron and Goldstein, *Hostage*, p. 8.

21. Ibid., pp. 222–26.

5

Culture Shock:

How Cultural Norms Can Keep an Organization in the Dark Even When Everything Else Has Changed

People in an organization frequently follow norms that have long since outlived their usefulness.[1]

Robert F. Allen and Frank J. Dyer

In the last chapter we discussed some of the dominant features of those personalities who are more likely to engage in unthinkable acts against corporations. In this chapter, we want to talk about the inner character—the culture—of those organizations that are most likely to deal effectively with the unthinkable or corporate tragedies of any sort. Thereby, we will be forming a bridge to the following chapters where we will be dealing explicitly with some methods for coping with the unthinkable.

The likelihood that an organization will anticipate and respond to an impending corporate tragedy is not just determined by the personality and intellectual capacity of its leaders. Nor is its responsiveness determined primarily by its corporate structure, its business policies, and incentive systems which make up its visible features. Rather, every organization also has an invisible quality, a certain style, a character, a way of doing things that may be more powerful than the dictates of any one person or any formal management system. To understand the essence or soul of an organization requires that we travel far beneath formal organization charts, rule books, employee manuals, machines, and buildings, into the underground world of corporate culture. This is where we will find the basis for an organization's stance toward the unthinkable.

The image of the world as simple machine would have us believe that a corporation's culture doesn't exist since it can't be seen or touched directly. The world as a complex system does not acknowledge the cultural aspects of an organization either since culture is not necessarily rational or logical. Culture taps the darker sides of human nature which allow for close-mindedness, denial, distortion, and spite—things that are not rational in the traditional sense of that term. The world as complex social network, however, recognizes the existence of culture explicitly, as an unconscious, hidden force that is deserving of study just because it is so pervasive and powerful. Culture allows us to examine the organization as a community, as a unique embodiment of such things as family conflict, gang warfare, crowd behavior, and alienation. Only a cultural conception comes close to capturing these dimensions of organizational life along with the more rational and mechanical aspects.

The study of the personalities of individuals has already gone through this progression from simple machine to complex social network, largely due to the pioneering work of Freud and Jung. It has only been recently that the study of organization culture has been taken seriously as a topic for systematic study.

Why has it taken so much longer to get at the essence of organizations than at the essence of individuals? As difficult as it has been to look at the darker side of humanity, perhaps there has always been the underlying hope that at least our organizations were good, pure, rational, and completely controllable—in short, the image of the organization as a simple machine. However, it can no longer be denied that our organizations are in deep trouble. For the first time in this century, the United States is not the worldwide leader in productivity. We have taken a back seat to Japan, West Germany, and perhaps other industrial nations as well. The late 1970s and early 1980s have witnessed a major economic recession if not depression. As a result, managers have had to take a hard look at themselves, their ways of managing, and their assumptions concerning the innermost qualities of the organization.

In the first part of this chapter we want to examine what corporate culture is and why it has such a strong hold over an organization, often without the consent of its members. What often ails an organization is an immense culture lag or culture gap. In many ways, the cultures of our dominant organizations still act as if they believe that nothing has changed, that which worked well in the past is still fine for today. Even stronger, cultures often work very hard at keeping everything the same, no matter what. Culture shock occurs when a sleeping organization awakes and finds that it has lost touch with its mission, its setting, and its assumptions. Rather than experience this shock, an unthinkable in its own right, many organizations "decide" not to wake up at all. Such organizations will be most susceptible to unthinkable acts from without as well as from within.

Last, we want to suggest how the cultural norms, or what we call the "unwritten rules of the game," of an organization can be brought to the surface for examination and for change. If an organization can do these things, then it is in a better position to gain control over the unspoken messages and tacit agreements that operate within it rather than vice versa. The members can decide on what new rules of behavior are needed for today's and tomorrow's problems. If they can do this, they can proceed to implement cultural change within their organization. We have the confidence that they can do this because we have participated directly in programs to make this happen, although we do not pretend it can happen easily.

WHAT IS CULTURE?

The culture of an organization is akin to a force field of energy. It is not mechanical, chemical, or electrical energy. Culture is best thought of as a social energy which has an existence and life all its own. The culture of an organization is distinct from its mission, its technologies, formal reward systems, explicit policies, and written job descriptions. While all these things may have been instrumental in shaping the initial culture, once formed, the culture becomes a separate force that controls members' behaviors and attitudes at the work place.

Operationally, culture is defined as a set of shared philosophies, ideologies, values, beliefs, expectations, attitudes, assumptions, and norms. Rarely are these intangibles of organizational life formally written down anywhere. Rather, they are learned by living in the organization and becoming a part of it. One has to experience the energy that flows from such shared understandings in order to know it.

Now a critical question is: Can management tap into this source of energy? Or, will it remain immobilized, unused, untapped? Or worse yet, can the energy be used against management and the goals of the organization? We have found that most organizations are not in control of their cultures. Rather, culture is the real director behind the scenes which actually runs the show. Often, organizations are fighting their past battles, reliving their dead traditions, acting out their no-longer-relevant assumptions of the business environment. In short, they wear social blinders. They are not able to see new ways of doing things, the need to be innovative, and to change directions. The culture simply won't allow for it. A top manager can call subordinates into his office, one by one, and get verbal commitments for some new policy or plan. He then finds that when each person leaves the office, and again becomes part of the corporate culture, the new plan is bitterly opposed, or even sabotaged.

We have found that culture can be managed and controlled. We will suggest how this can be done after we first examine the specific manifestations of culture—norms—and how these develop.

CULTURAL NORMS

Social scientists speak of norms as the unwritten rules which guide behavior.[2] For example, a typical norm in many organizations is: "Don't disagree with the boss." Such norms can exert a considerable hold on an organization. This occurs when a strong consensus exists among a group of people concerning what is appropriate behavior. If a certain norm is violated—if someone behaves differently than the norm dictates—then there are immediate and strong pressures to get the offending party to change his or her behavior. In the example above, consider an individual who, at a group meeting, persists in presenting his reservations concerning a new product the company is planning to introduce just after his boss had argued strongly for investing heavily in an advertising campaign for the new product. The individual in this situation would be stared at, frowned at, looked at with rolling eyes, as well as given nonverbal messages to sit down and shut up. If these efforts did not silence the individual, he would hear about it later, from his coworkers, or from his boss during his annual review.

 Every person's need to be accepted by a group—whether family, friends, coworkers, or one's neighborhood—gives a group incredible leverage to demand strong compliance with its norms. If people did not care about membership in a group at all, then a group would have little hold over individuals without any formal sanctions. The "rugged individualists," the nonconformists, the mavericks, and as we saw in the last chapter, psychopaths, are the only ones who seem to defy pressures to adhere to group norms—but always at a considerable price.

To give an example of just how powerfully a group can influence its members, consider the results of a simple experiment conducted by Solomon Asch in the 1950s.[3] The experiment was presented to subjects as a study solely in visual perception. Three lines, A, B and C, all of noticeably different lengths, were shown on a single card. Subjects were asked to indicate which of these three lines was identical in length to a fourth line D, shown on a second card. Seven persons sat in a row. One by one they indicated their choice. While line D was in fact identical to line C, each of the first six persons, confederates of the experimenter, said that line D was identical to A! Only the seventh person was the unknowing subject who was not part of the deception. As each person responded in turn to the experimenter's request, this seventh subject became increasingly uneasy, anxious, and doubtful of his own perceptions. When it was his turn to respond, this seventh subject agreed with the rest of the individuals 40 percent of the time. The error rate in choosing the wrong line without any other individuals present was less than 1 percent. Quite a difference in behavior! This simple experiment shows that there was nothing wrong with the eyes of the subjects. Rather, what the seventh subject reported he saw was strongly influenced by the opinions of the others.

In this experiment which has been duplicated many times, there wasn't any opportunity to discuss the problem among the seven persons. If there were such an opportunity, the effect would be even stronger. The six would attempt to influence the seventh member. It's not easy being a deviant in a group with everyone else against you. People need acceptance from others, as mentioned earlier. As a result, they will even deny their own perceptions when confronted with the group's norms of what is the "objective" reality. *Objective* reality becomes a *social* reality.

Another experiment, this time a study in an industrial plant, sheds further light on the nature of cultural norms. Also done in the 1950s, Stanley Seashore studied the effect of group cohesiveness on work performance.[4] Groups were found to vary on whether or not their norms supported company goals. That is, do the norms of the group encourage high levels of production or do the norms favor low production and doing the minimum to get by. The study found that the best condition for the organization was having highly cohesive groups with norms that support company goals. These groups did in fact achieve the highest levels of output. The worst condition was having highly cohesive groups with norms unsupportive or even against company goals. Here the groups used their social energy to keep output levels low. The uncohesive groups were intermediate in performance, regardless of their norms. In this case, individuals were left on their own to decide how much to produce since the impact of work group norms on their behavior was minimal.

HOW DO CULTURAL NORMS FORM?

Cultural norms seem to form rather quickly based upon the work setting and a few critical actions by key individuals. In a new organization, the business environment and the nature of the work to be done play a major role in shaping behavior. The formal reward systems, policies, procedures, and rules governing work, also have an impact on forming the initial culture. In addition, the personality, style, and actions of the founder and his top management staff contribute significantly to the cultural norms that are first set in motion.

More than anything else, however, people seem to remember a critical incident—like the time that so-and-so was reprimanded for doing a good job just because she wasn't asked to do it beforehand; or, so-and-so was fired because he disagreed with the company's position in public even though his arguments were sound and well presented. Incidents such as these become the folklore that people remember, indicating what the corporation *really* wants, what *really* counts in order to get ahead, or alternatively, how to stay out of trouble—the unwritten rules of the game. Work groups adopt these lessons as norms on how to survive and make it, how to protect oneself from the system, and how to retaliate against the organization for its "sins of the past."

A culture may be very functional at first, but over time, the culture becomes a separate social entity, independent of the initial reasons and incidents which formed it. As long as it is the same as the firm's documented systems and is supportive of them, the culture remains in the background. When management attempts to shift the goals of the corporation or tries to adopt new work methods, the cultural norms may not support the intended changes. Now the power and separateness of the culture will become evident very quickly. The intangible quality of the culture gets revealed as management can not pinpoint the source of apathy, resistance, or rebellion. Management is puzzled why the new work methods are not embraced automatically by the members. To management, it is so "obvious" how these proposed changes are for the good of the organization. Why can't everyone else see this?

Management is also caught in the grip of its own culture. Employees from below wonder why management plays it so safe, why they refuse to approach things differently, why they keep applying the same old management methods and styles even though these simply do not work. Employees wonder why management is so blind to the world around them. They wonder if management is mean or just stupid.

ASSESSING AND CHANGING CULTURAL NORMS

How can we find out what the current culture is and, in particular, whether the current culture supports the objectives of the firm? Perhaps even more central to our concerns, does the current culture foster a proactive stance toward the unthinkable both inside and outside the organization? Alternatively, does the current culture serve to prevent the membership of the organization from even contemplating the unthinkable?

Members can be asked to verbalize and write out what previously was unwritten. We have done this many times with a variety of organizations. We have found that members are willing and able to write out their norms under certain conditions. The right conditions include: no member will be identified for stating or suggesting a particular norm (individual confidentiality), and that no norm is documented when one's superiors are present (candid openness). Further, the members have to trust that the "norm list" will not be used against them. Instead, the listing of norms will be used to benefit them as well as the whole organization and society. The consultant or facilitator who guides members to state norms, therefore, must generate trust and commitment.

Step One: Surfacing Current Norms

The first step is to ask members (generally in a workshop setting) what norms currently guide their behaviors and attitudes. Sometimes it takes a little prodding and a few illustrations to get the process started. Once it begins, members are quick to suggest norms. In fact, we have found that they seem to delight in being able to articulate what beforehand was never stated in any document or rarely mentioned in any conversation.

For an organization whose culture is rooted deeply in the past, some of the norms that get listed are: Don't disagree with your boss; don't rock the boat; treat women as second-class citizens; downgrade your organization; don't enjoy your work; don't share information with other groups; treat subordinates as incompetent and lazy; cheat on your expense account; look busy even when you are not; don't reward employees based on merit; laugh at those who suggest new ways of doing things; don't smile much; openly criticize company policies to outsiders; complain a lot; don't trust anyone who seems sincere. Ironically, the one norm that has to be violated so that this list can be developed is: don't make norms explicit!

Norms that get listed which directly pertain to unthinkable and difficult problems are: Don't be the bearer of bad news; don't tell your boss what he doesn't want to hear; don't think of things that are not likely to happen; don't spoil the party; don't be associated with an ugly event; see no evil, hear no evil, and speak no evil.

As these norms are listed on a flip chart for everyone to see, there is usually considerable laughter and amazement. The members become aware that they have been seducing one another to abide by these counterproductive directives. But it is not that each individual made a conscious choice to behave this way. Rather, as each individual entered the organization, each was taught what is expected behavior—often in very subtle ways. The more cohesive the group, the more rapidly this learning took place and the more strongly the sanctions were applied. In the extreme case, a highly cohesive group that has been around a long time has members that look, act, think, and talk like one another.

It is the power that the group has over the individual—compliance to group norms in exchange for group membership—that makes the negative focus of the norms so critical and potentially devastating.[5] What makes matters worse, is that individuals go along with group norms rather automatically without questioning the consequences, either for themselves or for their organization. We have found that the "decision process," if one can call it that, is largely unconscious. Individuals do not decide on a day-by-day basis to enact the negative and unproductive norms. Rarely are the cultural norms discussed openly nor are they written down anywhere for open inspection. They simply evolve.

In the projects where we have had the managers and all the employees of a company list their norms, it is surprising to discover the high proportion of negative norms that are cited. In a number of cases, more than 90 percent of the listed norms have mildly negative or even highly negative connotations. It might be that these members felt we were looking for the dysfunctions in their organizations rather than the positive and functional aspects. On the other hand, perhaps many organizations are plagued with a high proportion of negative norms, the kind that were listed above.

Interestingly, we have found that left to itself, a culture tends to become negative. Human fear, insecurity, sensitivity, dependency, and paranoia seem to take over unless a concerted effort at establishing positive norms is undertaken. As we discussed in the previous chapter, most people have been hurt at one time or another in their lives, particularly in childhood. It is, therefore, rather easy to scare people into worrying about what pain or hurt will be inflicted in the future, even in a relatively nonthreatening situation. As a result, people cope by protecting themselves, by being cautious, by minimizing their risks, by going along with the negative, self-protecting group norms. A positive set of norms, alternatively, requires a risk-taking, proactive, independent, and stimulus-seeking approach to organizational as well as individual life. The latter only can be accomplished by a deliberate, conscious, well-planned effort at culture management.

Step Two: Determining New Directions

The next step in the process of gaining control over the culture is to discuss: Where is the organization or work group headed; what innovations need to be adopted; what type of behavior is necessary to implement these new work methods? Even when a corporation has a very dysfunctional culture from the past, members, as individuals, are aware of what changes are needed for the organization to survive and be effective in the future. Members are aware, similarly, of what work environment they prefer for their own sanity and satisfaction. It is the culture that holds everyone back.

Oftentimes, a certain amount of planning and problem solving have to occur before any new directions can be articulated. For work groups that have been in a culture rut, members have been so absorbed with the negatives that they have not spent much time thinking about or discussing what the positive would be like. Sometimes it is helpful to ask them as individuals or as a group, to consider their ideal organization.[6] That is, if they could design their own organization from scratch, what would it be like? This generally brings to life what could be different in the present organization and what shouldn't be assumed just because it has been this way for a long period of time.

In the case where some form of strategic planning is necessary before future directions of the firm can be stated, then a more elaborate process may be necessary. Representatives from various groups might share their different scenarios for the future directions of the organization. Examining the different stakeholders that may be affected by these plans including the assumptions that support each person's or group's position, is likely to generate a lively discussion and debate on what the future should bring.[7] The following chapters say more about this method for coping with difficult and complex problems, whether they be strategic planning or the unthinkable.

Step Three: Establishing New Norms

The third step in the process is for the members to develop a list of new norms that would support their desires for change. For example, what new norms would encourage a more proactive stance toward the organization's changing environment? Likewise, what new norms would allow groups to discuss difficult and uncomfortable issues that affect the long-term survival and success of the firm? What cultural norms would bring the unthinkables out into the open so they can be anticipated and resolved when possible?

At this point the members usually catch on to the impact that the unwritten rules have had on their behavior. They experience a sense of relief as a new way of life is considered. They realize that they no longer have to pressure one another to behave in dysfunctional ways. The members can create a new social order within their own work groups, within their own organization. Part of this sense of relief is recognizing that their dissatisfactions and being ineffective do not derive from their being incompetent or bad individuals. It is much easier and perhaps more comfortable, psychologically, to blame the invisible force called culture, as long as they take responsibility for changing it.

For organizations needing to be more adaptive, flexible, and responsive to modern times, some of the norms that get listed are: Treat everyone with respect and as a potential source of valuable insights and expertise; be willing to take on responsibility; initiate changes to improve performance; congratulate those who suggest new ideas and new ways of doing things; be cost conscious so that the organization remains efficient relative to its competitors; speak with pride about your organization and work group; budget your time according to the importance of tasks for the accomplishment of objectives; don't criticize the organization in front of clients or customers; enjoy your work and show your enthusiasm for a job well done; be helpful and supportive of the other groups in the organization.

New norms that directly pertain to the unthinkable include: Bring uncomfortable issues out into the open; persist in drawing attention to problems even if others seem reluctant to consider the implications of what you are saying; listen to other members' viewpoints even if you disagree with them; encourage zany and bizarre perspectives to assure that nothing important or possible has been overlooked; take notice if there hasn't been a strong difference of opinion on a topic that should generate a heated debate.

Step Four: Identifying Culture-Gaps

The contrast between these desired norms (Step Three) and the actual norms (Step One) can be immense. The second author and a colleague, Mary J. Saxton, are referring to this contrast as a culture-gap. They have developed a measurement tool for detecting culture problems, the gap between what the current culture is and what it should be. The Kilmann-Saxton Culture-Gap Survey,[8] as it is called, also sets the stage for a program for changing a culture—from one which is troubled and off track to one which will be effective and on track.

The survey diagnoses the extent and source of culture problems for any company or organization. The survey has 28 norm pairs. Most of these norms have been mentioned repeatedly in Step One and Step Three of our studies. An example is: A. Share information only when it benefits your own work group, vs. B. Share information to foster overall effective decision making. Each employee chooses the *A* or *B* for each norm pair in two ways: First, according to the pressures the work group puts on its members (actual norms) and second, according to which norms should be operating in order to promote high performance and morale (desired norms).

The differences between the actual norms and the desired norms represent the culture-gaps. There are four types of culture-gaps, each made up of seven norm pairs:

1. Task Support—norms having to do with information sharing, helping other groups, concern with efficiency, e.g., "Support the work of other groups" vs. "Ridicule the work of other groups."

2. Task Innovation—norms for being creative, being rewarded for creativity, doing new things, e.g., "Always try to improve" vs. "Don't rock the boat."
3. Social Relationships—norms for socializing with your work group, mixing friendships with business, e.g., "Get to know the people in your work group" vs. "Don't bother."
4. Personal Freedom—norms for self-expression, exercising discretion, pleasing yourself, e.g., "Live for yourself and your family" vs. "Live for your job and career."

Using the Kilmann-Saxton Culture-Gap Survey in numerous profit and nonprofit organizations has revealed distinct patterns of culture-gaps.[9] For example, in some of the high technology firms, lack of cooperation and information sharing across groups have resulted in large culture-gaps in Task Support. In the automotive and steel industries, not rewarding creativity and innovation have resulted in large culture-gaps in Task Innovation. In some social service agencies, where work loads can vary greatly, large gaps in Social Relationships are found indicating that too much time is spent socializing rather than looking to get the next job done. Last, in extremely bureaucratic organizations, such as some banks and government agencies, large gaps in Personal Freedom are evident. Here members feel overly confined and constrained which affects their performance and morale.

The most general finding to date, however, is large culture-gaps in Task Innovation. It seems that U.S. industry is plagued by significant differences between actual and desired norms in this area. This is consistent with all the attention that has been given to the productivity problem in the United States. An industrial culture that pushes short-term financial results is bound to foster norms against efforts at long-term work improvements regardless of what the formal documents seem to advocate.

Step 5: Closing the Culture-Gap

How can the culture-gaps be closed? How can a corporation move its culture from the actual to the desired? Can a company be taken out of a culture rut and be put back on track for solving present and future problems? Will the organization survive this culture shock?

When the current culture is at least hopeful, it is almost miraculous what impact the survey results or a listing of the desired norms has on the members of a work unit. As mentioned before, there is often a great sense of relief as people become aware that they can live according to different norms and that they have *the power to change.* Surprisingly, some change from the actual to the desired norms can take place just by listing the new set of norms. Members start "playing out" the new norms soon after these are discussed. They survive the shock.

When the current culture is cynical, depressed, and in a deep rut, the response to the survey results is quite different. Even when large gaps are shown or when a listing demonstrates the tremendous differences between actual and desired norms, the members seem apathetic and lifeless. Members respond by saying that their work units cannot change for the better until the level of management above them and the rest of the company change first. Members believe that it is the external "system" that is keeping them down.

Curiously, when we do a culture-gap survey at the next highest level, the very same arguments are heard again: "We have no power to change; we have to wait for the next level to let us change; they have the power!" It is shocking to conduct the culture-gap survey for an entire organization, to present the results to the top management group, only to find the same feelings of apathy and helplessness. Here top management is waiting for the economy to change. In actuality, it is the corporate culture that is saying: "Don't take on responsibility; protect yourself at all costs; don't try to change until everyone else has changed; don't lead the way, follow; if you ignore the problem, maybe it will go away."

This is the perfect example of a company in a culture rut, where the shock of realizing the discrepancy between actual and desired norms is just too great to confront. Instead, the organization buries its head in the sand and hopes everything will be sorted out by itself. Even in the face of strong evidence of a serious problem, time and time again we have witnessed this form of organizational denial—a much more powerful and perhaps destructive force than any case of individual denial. The group's power to define reality, clouds each person's better judgment. The undiscussed culture "wins" again.

One company in the top 50 of the *Fortune 500* asked us to present a three-day seminar to the top executive group (the chairman of the board and chief operating officer, and the top 10 corporate officers) on the topic of corporate culture. Rather than just present abstract ideas concerning why culture is important, we suggested that a representative survey of culture-gaps be conducted across all divisions of the company. In a couple of weeks, the vice president of human resources got back to us with his response: "No, we better not do this. I don't think the executive group really wants to know what is going on in the company. Besides, we can't take the chance of surprising them with your survey results." Who's protecting whom?

At another meeting with a top 50 company on the same topic, we shared the above anecdote as an example of the U.S. culture problem without, of course, mentioning any names. The response to our story was: "That must be our company you're talking about!" It wasn't. But the message is still the same.

A major lesson to learn from changing corporate cultures, especially dysfunctional and depressed cultures—those in a culture rut—is that people do not have to feel powerless and inept. If managers and members decide that taking on responsibility for change and feeling the power to change should be part of the new culture, then it can be done. *Power and control are more a matter of social perception than they are of objective, physical reality.* Many times individuals and organizations have moved forward and achieved great success when everyone else "knew" that it was impossible for them to do so.

Merely listing and stating new norms, however, is not enough to instill them throughout an organization. Also, norms cannot be altered by just requesting them to change. Members have to develop agreements that the new norms will indeed replace the old norms, and that this change will be monitored and sanctioned by the work groups. Specifically, among the questions to be answered are: How will members reinforce one another for enacting the new behaviors and attitudes; how will members confront one another when the old set of norms creeps back into the work group; how can the leadership of the group reward members who foster the new culture; can any aspects of formal management system, such as performance appraisal, be altered to support the development of the new culture; how will management accept a change in the culture and will they begin to question their own ideology and values; can members show management the benefits of supporting the cultural change?

For example, consider a new norm: Congratulate those who suggest new ideas and new ways of doing things. If any member notices that a coworker frowns when some new product idea is suggested, the coworker would be given suitable stares and reminders of the new norms. He may even be confronted with some statement as: "I thought you were part of the team and had agreed to make the switch. What's your problem?"

If any corporation determined the extent of its culture-gaps using the aforementioned steps, it would be in a position to chart directions for a cultural change. Conducting sessions for each division, department, and work group, including the ways in which the new norms will be monitored and enforced, would begin the change process. If top management were committed to such a cultural change then it could institutionalize the change. Formal control and incentive systems would be adapted to monitor and reward behavior that reflected the new norms. Now the formal management and organizational systems would be working with the informal, intangible work-group pressures to move the corporation in the desired direction. The social energy of the members would be behind the organization.

CULTURES FOR COPING WITH THE UNTHINKABLE

Getting control of a corporation's culture is not only possible but it is necessary for the turbulent times that contemporary organizations now face. As changes in corporate directions are planned and implemented, a new culture may have to replace the old culture—in one or more divisions or for the whole of the organization. But just as old cultures can become out-of-date and dysfunctional, the same can happen with any new culture. Further changes in the business environment, the development of technology, the structure of jobs, and the characteristics of new members, can make any culture less functional than before. An important part of controlling a corporation's culture, therefore, is to continue the monitoring and assessment of norms. This is what is meant by "culture management." Culture is subject to decision making and action taking just like any other management problem.

The importance of managing culture should be even more evident when we consider the growing intrusion of evil forces into corporate life. Criminal acts against organizations are increasing dramatically. Coping with this, and thus managing it, is a problem that bears especially on the culture of an organization. Essentially, we have to question whether the culture of most organizations will let members acknowledge this, let alone allow them to confront the reality of it directly. If most of U.S. industry is in a culture rut or at least has serious culture problems, how can our corporations learn to appreciate and act upon this new development? Our organizations have enough trouble just being productive in the traditional sense.

One message however should be clear. Neither government, the board of directors, nor any top management group of a corporation can hope to legislate coping with unthinkable acts by changes in formal objectives, written policies, procedures, or incentives alone. Creating a new group in charge of "the problem" is not likely to work either. The group's recommendations will fall on deaf ears. What is necessary is nothing short of a dramatic shift in the culture of a corporation, from one that suppresses bad news of any type to one that actively looks for different viewpoints, opinions, and contradictory information. Further, the new culture has to encourage all members to state their views candidly and openly without fear of discussing taboo subjects, and without fear of any reprisal. A method for doing this once an organization has committed to it is the topic of the next two chapters.

Our own view is that the type of culture that would support a proactive stance toward anticipating corporate tragedies and acting upon them quickly is the same kind of culture that is necessary for addressing any of the truly complex problems corporations now face. Indeed, how could it be any different? There is a critical need to bring as much information as possible to bear on the problem by considering as many diverse viewpoints as possible. Anything that gets members to withhold information or suppress any creative ideas or approaches is, potentially, deadly— literally! We can't let formal incentive systems that breed competition or departmental structures that foster a loyalty to a narrow perspective, get in the way of complex problem solving. We can't let the old approaches to simple problems—problems which easily can be assigned to one person or one group—be applied to an altogether different type of world, the world as complex social network rather than the world as simple machine.

If the culture of our organizations can't cope with unthinkable acts and corporate tragedies then, in all likelihood, they really can't cope with any important, complex problem. It would just be a matter of time before something unthinkable or tragic does them in. Ironically, it probably wouldn't be a tragedy per se; it would most likely be a culture that has kept the organization in the dark when everything else around it has changed.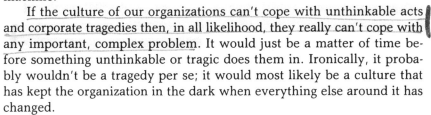

NOTES

1. Robert F. Allen and Frank J. Dyer, "A Tool for Tapping the Organizational Unconscious," *Personnel Journal,* March 1980, p. 192.

2. Jay M. Jackson, "Structural Characteristics of Norms," in *The Dynamics of Instructional Groups: Socio-Psychological Aspects of Teaching and Learning,* ed. M.B. Henry (Chicago: University of Chicago Press, 1960), chap. 7. For the most up-to-date and comprehensive discussion on group norms, see: Michael Moch and Stanley E. Seashore, "How Norms Affect Behaviors In and Of Corporations" in *Handbook of Organizational Design,* ed. Paul C. Nystrom and William H. Starbuck (London: Oxford University Press, 1981), pp. 210-37.

3. Solomon E. Asch, "Opinions and Social Pressure," *Scientific American,* November 1955, pp. 31-34. Also see: Richard S. Crutchfield, "Conformity and Character," *American Psychologist* 10 (1955): 191-98.

4. Stanley E. Seashore, *Group Cohesiveness in the Industrial Work Group* (Ann Arbor, Mich.: Institute for Social Research, 1954).

5. Robert F. Allen and Charlotte Kraft, *The Organizational Unconscious: How to Create the Corporate Culture You Want and Need* (Englewood Cliffs, N.J.: Prentice-Hall, 1982), for a fuller treatment of negative and dsyfunctional norms and their impact on organizations.

6. Ian I. Mitroff and Ralph H. Kilmann, "Stories Managers Tell: A New Tool for Organizational Problem Solving," *Management Review,* July 1975, pp. 18-28.

7. Ian I. Mitroff, Ralph H. Kilmann, and Vincent P. Barabba, "The Application of Behavioral and Philosophical Technologies to Strategic Planning: A Case Study With a Large Federal Agency," *Management Science* 24, (1977):44-58.

8. Ralph K. Kilmann and Mary J. Saxton, *Kilmann-Saxton Culture-Gap Survey* (Pittsburgh: Organizational Design Consultants, 1983).

9. Ralph H. Kilmann, *Beyond the Quick Fix: Managing Five Tracks to Organizational Success* (San Francisco: Jossey-Bass, 1984).

6

Coping I:
Elementary Coping

What American industry has to learn from the Japanese is not to be learned through inflating the value of their example. The proper lesson is of a different sort. What the Japanese have done is to build an approach to the work of manufacturing that takes explicitly and centrally into account the realities of the new industrial competition. By contrast, American managers too often view their work through a haze of outdated assumptions and expectations.[1]

> William J. Abernathy,
> Kim B. Clark, and
> Alan M. Kantrow

INTRODUCTION

In this and the next chapter, we want finally to turn our attention to the central question behind this entire book: What can one do to cope more effectively with the kinds of unthinkable, tragic acts that have been happening to corporations? The time has finally come to present the broad outlines of a (not, *the*) method for coping with the unthinkable.

This chapter presents the broad outline of a general method for thinking about inordinately complex, messy, real-world problems. It represents our attempt to fashion a method of thinking that is applicable to the kinds of problems that are rampant in today's world. While the technique can be used for exercises as well, it was not fashioned with them in mind. It was fashioned in an attempt to address itself to all of the difficulties and shortcomings of today's problem-solving techniques that were mentioned in earlier chapters.

This chapter presents the broad outlines of the general method. The method is presented in terms of a real-world case that, as we shall shortly see, is even more pertinent today to the subject matter of this book than when it was first encountered. The next chapter shows how the general concepts of this chapter can be modified and how they need to be extended to address themselves explicitly to each of the separate types of corporate tragedies that were discussed in the first chapter.

THE CASE OF THE DRUG COMPANY

Imagine that you are the chief executive of a large organization and that you are faced with a problem which threatens in one blow to wipe out your entire business. This is a problem that would certainly command your attention.

The problem is this (actually, as we shall see, there are several levels to "the problem"): you produce a product, a painkiller, which because it has a narcotic base can only be obtained by prescription through a physician. Upon obtaining the prescription for your drug, a well-known brand-name product, the patient takes it to his or her favorite pharmacist. The pharmacist in turn either fills the prescription without comment as instructed by the physician or says something to the patient like, "Did you know that there is a generic-brand substitute available for the drug your physician has prescribed at a much lower cost than the brand name? If you like, I can substitute the cheaper generic brand for the more expensive brand label. Which do you prefer I do?" And in some states, the pharmacist is required by law to inform the patient explicitly that there is an available generic substitute.

This action, while potentially beneficial to the patient, assuming that the generic-brand drug is of equal quality to the name-brand drug, is a potential financial disaster for the drug company. It threatens to wipe out in one dramatic blow one of the mainstay products of the company. Since the drug annually generates millions of dollars for the company, the company's whole financial structure is threatened as a result. What do you as the chief executive officer do?

You can do a number of things. You can attempt to think the problem through yourself, taking the whole burden upon yourself, either not delegating it to anyone else or not trusting it to them. You can then attempt to choose on your own the best option open to you to combat the threat. Or you can do something else which, depending how it is done, can either replace or supplement the first alternative of going it by yourself. This is to involve others in the analysis of the problem. Since the problem threatens financial disaster for the whole organization, it might be desirable to involve others in a consideration of their own fate for the good of the whole. Also, it just might be that more heads are better than one in coming up with needed and creative alternatives, especially in a crisis situation when critical faculties are likely to be blunted and stressed. No single mind—except God's—can ever know all there is to know about any complex organization. It is the height of folly and delusion to fool oneself into thinking that one can. The final decision will still be yours but if you have the right style of corporate culture, this need not preclude participation by others in the analysis of the problem and perhaps even in the final decision. Certainly you would like others to go along with whatever you decide and not to sabotage it.

In this authentic case the chief executive decided to involve some of his senior executives in the analysis of the problem. Because of the critical nature of the problem, it literally affected every aspect of the business. As a result, the chief executive officer (C.E.O.) felt that he had no choice but to solicit the most widespread expert advice from as many different aspects of the organization as possible. He also welcomed such diversity for the problem was too critical not to consult with others. As a consequence, twelve or so key executives representing all of the diverse aspects of the business were assembled and asked to advise the C.E.O. Here is precisely where the deeper and more interesting aspects of the problem began to emerge.

A strange thing began to happen. The twelve executives split into three subfactions. This was not done out of any animosity between them, but because complex problems naturally suggest more than one "best" alternative. The senior executives began to coalesce around the particular alternative that individually made best sense to them. Each group then proceeded to make the best, i.e., strongest, case for its alternative to the exclusion of the other two.

The three alternatives were as follows: the first group wanted to lower the price of the drug; the second wanted to raise the price; and the third wanted to keep it the same. The first group in effect wanted to "out-generic" the generic drug by making the company's drug into a generic, at least in terms of price. This alternative or policy is the one that most easily occurs to anyone. It is in many ways a defensive policy. This doesn't necessarily make it "wrong," for as we have stressed, in complex real-world problems there are not always clear right or wrong answers. Some responses may be stronger than others along some grounds but very rarely is one alternative strongest or best on all dimensions.

The second alternative is the diametric opposite of the first. Furthermore, it shows that in the realm of complex problems not only is there usually more than one serious alternative, but further still, that there is generally at least one pair of alternatives such that each one of the pair is the complete opposite of the other. Thus, in the case at hand, alternative two is the complete opposite of alternative one.

The reasoning behind alternative two is even more fascinating and important for our purposes. The group of executives that supported this alternative argued that faced with the threat of generic drugs they had to do something which would communicate to the marketplace the difference between their drug and the others. They had in short to differentiate themselves from the mass of other products. This group felt that by raising the price of the drug they would be communicating increased confidence in the *quality* of their product to the marketplace. They were thus making an important and largely unstated assumption about consumer psychology, i.e., that some people will buy a product if its perceived quality, as signaled through a greater price, is high.

The last group argued something entirely different. While the first two groups were oriented toward the external marketplace and the price consumers would be willing to pay or to bear, the last group was oriented toward cutting internal costs of production. They argued that if the price of the drug were maintained at current levels, or at the very least, set midway between the proposals of the first two groups, then they could raise profits by cutting internal costs. They proposed to do this by eliminating the Research and Development (R & D) arm of the company, the largest source of internal costs to the company and perhaps to drug companies in general. Their argument was that if the current price of the drug was sufficient to generate necessary revenue for the company, that is if the demand for the drug remained stable, then the company would not need to develop new products. To say the least, the R & D department as a critical stakeholder in the company wouldn't be overjoyed with this, but then business was business, or at least as this group saw it.

Since each group was of roughly equal power in the organization, no group could force through its pet alternative over the objections of the others. Each group had to convince all the groups if the company was to embark on a unified course of action that everyone could embrace with confidence.

How then did each of the groups try to persuade one another of the correctness of their individual policy? They did what most managers have been trained to do. They analyzed past data, e.g., past sales volume (amount sold) for various selling prices of the drug, and where they could, they collected new data, e.g., from trade magazines and reports from salespeople from the field. The trouble was, in this case at least, that the data didn't settle anything. They actually made things worse. They only convinced the proponents even more of the truth of their separate policies. The reason for this may be the most illuminating and instructive aspect of the entire problem.

One of the valuable things we learn in school is to test our ideas against the criticisms of others, and wherever possible, challenging data from the outside world. In school this tactic generally succeeds because,

as we pointed out in Chapter 2, the kinds of problems that are presented
to the student are so greatly simplified; i.e., they are exercises and not
really problems at all.

In this case, more data merely confounded the "mess" with which
management was faced. Indeed "mess" is a more appropriate word to
use in describing this case than the more benign word "problem."
Ackoff[2] defines a "mess" as a *system* of problems none of which can be
formulated independently from one another, let alone solved independently of all the other problems on which it impacts and which impact
on it. In addition, each group was assuming different things about the
nature of the problem. Each group was taking certain things for
granted—to be true—without conscious or explicit knowledge that they
were doing this.

As a result, each group was selectively reinterpreting the data they
did have in common, unconsciously of course, to suit, if not prove, its
own particular case. Further, where past data in common were not available and hence where they had to go out and collect new data, each group
was collecting different data from different sources. Each source was
designed, again largely unconsciously, to prove each group's individual
case. Hence, *instead of data really testing each alternative, each alternative*
was being used to direct its believers into procuring data that would confirm
the validity of its alternative. A very circular process indeed and one from
which management had tried repeatedly, without success, to extricate itself. But since everything depended upon which assumptions were made,
as in fact every complex problem in the real world does, the case couldn't
be analyzed without making some very important critical assumptions.
But since very few, if any, of the critical assumptions were ever raised
to the surface for conscious inspection and challenge, each group cycled
around its own vicious circle.

Not that management didn't try to break out of this circle. They used
every financial model and approach of which they were aware in an attempt to get some neutral piece of data or critical finding that would once
and for all clearly differentiate between them. However much they tried,
time and again their expectations were dashed.

It was at this point that Mitroff and a colleague, James Emshoff, entered the scene in the role of consultants. For years, Emshoff and the
authors had worked on problems of this kind independently of one another. A year's visiting appointment for Mitroff at the Wharton School
of Finance, University of Pennsylvania, gave us the opportunity to combine our insights. As a result of this collaboration, we achieved what for
all of us was a real "breakthrough" (a much overused word) in formulating a method for handling problems of the kind we have been describing. We were able to formulate in practical and operational terms a via-

ble method for handling complex messy problems. Since the method has been described extensively elsewhere, we shall merely review it here.[3]

ASSUMPTION ANALYSIS

It soon became clear to Emshoff and Mitroff that differences in basic assumptions were at the heart of the disagreement among the groups. Each group was making a fundamentally different set of assumptions about the "real nature of the problem." No wonder why more data didn't settle anything between them. More data only served to activate underlying differences. It didn't test or resolve them. It only made things worse. We have a perfect example of where "more can lead to less." Since for the most part the assumptions remained buried and implicit, the groups themselves were largely unaware of what was happening. All they knew was that time and again they disagreed and were immensely frustrated.

How then could we get the participants to reveal to us and to themselves in a nonthreatening way the underlying assumptions that were driving their policies? *Assumptions are like the weather. Everyone talks about them, their influence, their crucial importance, but after that, no one offers a way of getting to them and for dealing with them.* This is what we were after. Having said this, we are not sure that Mitroff and Emshoff were themselves fully aware of what they were fashioning in the initial meetings with the drug company executives but it soon began to dawn on them.

It turned out that both Emshoff and the authors had for some time been working with a concept that was a bare stone's throw away from assumptions. This is the concept of *stakeholders* that we discussed in Chapter 2.

Figure 6-1 shows a broader stakeholder map of the drug company. This figure is similar in spirit to Figure 2-2 in Chapter 2.

Notice that a double line of influence extends from each stakeholder to the organization and back again. This is because *an organization is the entire set of relationships it has with itself and its stakeholders.* An organization is not a physical "thing" per se but a series of social and institutional relationships between a wide series of parties. As these relationships change over time, the organization itself may be thought of as changing, as becoming a different organization. The failure to grasp this essential fact has prevented many an organization from seeing that it is not the same because its environment, i.e., its external stakeholders, has changed even though internally it looks the same to itself. Since we are dealing with a system, a change in any one part *potentially* affects all other parts and the whole system itself.[4]

FIGURE 6-1

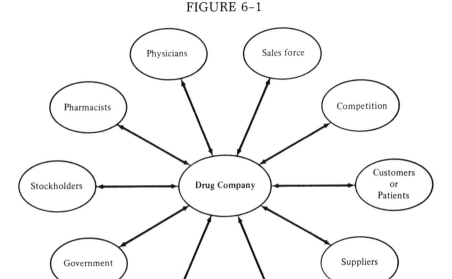

An Expanded Stakeholder Map

Let's examine Figure 6-1 a bit further to see its implications. Every organization has some form of external competition. While not formally a part of the inside of the organization, it affects the organization and its policies nonetheless. Every organization must ask itself such questions as: "If we do such and such, what will our competition do? If we enter this market, will our competition grow, leave, retaliate? Who is our current competition? How determined, how strong are they? What might our future competition be? Can we prevent our competition from entering our turf, our market in the first place? Can we raise the 'entry costs' (e.g., capital accumulation) high enough to keep them out or at least block their easy entry? If we decide for whatever reasons to get out of a particular market, can we do it in such a way as to make it more difficult for our competition to get out of a worsening situation? If we get out first, will it be more difficult for others to get out later?" These questions are so important that an exciting, new, major school of business policy and planning has arisen recently to consider them explicitly.[5]

Competition is certainly an important factor in the present case since it was the explicit competitive threat from lower-price generic drugs that started the whole crisis in the first place. But so are all the other stakeholder parties as well. The company's sales force are an important stakeholder since whatever policy the company enacts potentially affects their commissions and hence their motivation to sell the drug. Physicians and pharmacists are also obviously important since it is they and not the drug company who have direct contact with the customers, the patient in this case. Their behavior, i.e., attitude toward the company and its products, is obviously an important factor in the patient's behavior.

Consider a few more stakeholders. Government is a stakeholder in this case in at least two important roles. First, it regulates through the Federal Drug Administration, the sale, release, testing, use, and distribution of drugs. This is especially the case where narcotics are involved. Second, since the drug has an important narcotic base, the government comes into the picture through the procurement and regulation of opiates from foreign countries. Things that happen in poppy fields a long way from home affect a drug company here in the United States.

Finally, consider the stakeholder, the holding company. The drug company in this case was owned by another larger pharmaceutical company 50 miles up the road, so to speak. They certainly had a stake in whatever the subsidiary decided to do for it would certainly affect the profits of the larger parent company.

What has all this got to do with assumptions? Simply put, *assumptions are the properties of stakeholders.* The proponents of the different policies in the drug company were disagreeing, often strongly, because they were positing very different properties about the behavior of the stakeholders. But why assumptions? Because no one had the definitive data, information, arguments, to know for sure beyond all doubt what all the stakeholders were like or likely to behave in all situations.

The bigger, the more complex the problem, the more it is likely to involve a wider array of stakeholder forces. The more, as a result, that assumptions will have to be made. It is a characteristic, fundamental feature of real-world, as opposed to textbook, problems that not everything of basic importance can be known prior to working on the problem. In the real world we do not start with a clear statement of the problem before we commence working on it. Rather, a statement of the problem often only emerges with difficulty over time and only as a direct result of our working on the problem. Very few problems come directly to us preformulated from the gods. Rather, they are intensely human creations that are born out of the process of what it means to be human, i.e., as a result of human interaction.[6]

At last we come to the crux of the problem. Consider the single stakeholder, the physician. It illustrates what was driving the groups apart.

And indeed, it turns out that the assumptions in regards to the physician were the most critical of all the assumptions that were being made. For ease of presentation, we shall consider only the two groups, the one that wanted to raise the price of the drug and the one that wanted to lower it. The group that wanted to raise the price was assuming implicitly that physicians were motivated primarily by the traditional model of medical care, i.e., that physicians were primarily concerned with the health and well-being of the patient *relatively irrespective of cost.* This group was assuming that physicians were relatively price-*insensitive* to the cost of the drug. Physicians would prescribe the drug if they thought it would do the job, i.e., if they were convinced of its quality; and if they did, a further assumption was that the physician's recommendation would be critical in overcoming the counter-suggestion of the pharmacist. As one can see, there are actually a whole bundle of assumptions tied up with the physician and his or her effect on other stakeholders such as the patient and the pharmacist.

The group, on the other hand, that wanted to lower the price of the drug was assuming implicitly that because of the skyrocketing cost of medical care, physicians were becoming greatly more cost conscious than ever before. In other words, physicians were becoming increasingly price-*sensitive.* They would no longer prescribe a drug merely because of its touted quality irrespective of its cost. At some point, quality, especially claimed superior quality, would have to give way to cost.

There was a special wrinkle that Emshoff and Mitroff introduced that especially made it possible for the different groups to be able to *see* their assumptions, let alone their effects. This was the introduction of a simple yet effective way of mapping or plotting assumptions. Figure 6–2 shows this.

Once the pertinent stakeholders have been identified and the assumptions associated with them have been surfaced, typically some assumptions are more critical or important to the success or viability of a policy than others. Likewise, one feels more confident about the truth or certainty of some assumptions than others. Thus, Figure 6–2 shows that all of the groups, but for very different reasons, regarded the physician as the most important but most uncertain stakeholder. Consider again the high-price group and understand that *it is the assumption with regard to the stakeholder, not the stakeholder itself, that is being plotted in Figure 6–2.* Thus, the assumption that "physicians are *price-insensitive*" is both the most critical (important) assumption to the success of the high-price group's policy, but when revealed, it is also the one that is the most uncertain. Without the assumption of price insensitivity this group's policy cannot fly, but at the same time it is the most open to doubt. Are *all* physicians price-insentive? Or merely *some?* But if so, what are the "some"

FIGURE 6-2

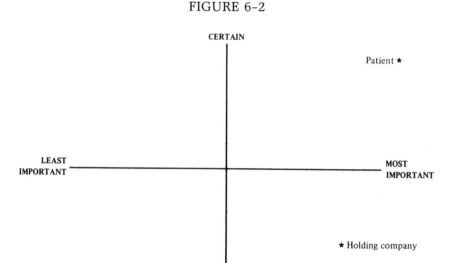

A Map of Stakeholder Assumptions

who are price-insensitive like? What are their personal and demographic characteristics? No wonder more data didn't settle anything because the data that were relevant to these questions were either unavailable—they had never been collected before—or they were ambiguous. One could infer whatever one wanted from the data because the data that were available were all "mixed up"; they contained data on physicians of all kinds.

The second most important and uncertain stakeholder was that of the holding company. If you go with raising the price, then you have to assume, as the high-price group did, that the holding company is primarily interested in maximizing profits. It will sell less of the drug (lower volume) but make more per drug sold. On the other hand, if you lower the price, you have to assume, as the low-price group did, that the holding company is primarily interested in maximizing market-share. You sell more of the drug (greater volume) but you make less per drug sold. You have to assume that the holding company is primarily interested in becoming the market-leader in its industry.

Neither assumption is necessarily wrong; they are merely different. Which one is best depends on the overall objectives of the parent company *and* the subsidiary drug company considered as a total *system*. Notice that although we started with just one part of the system, the drug company, we have ended up having to consider the whole system. This is in itself one of the prime features of complex problems. They involve or turn into a whole systems problem.[7]

If the assumption involving the parent holding company was so important, one might ask, "Why didn't the drug company merely call up or visit its 'parent' so close by?" The answer is, "If only organization politics and jockeying for power, prestige, and influence were that simple!" Just to ask for clarification of something in some systems is not as simple as it may appear. Nor is it necessarily rewarded by those "on top" who may not know the answers themselves and as a result do not want to reveal their ignorance. In short the culture of the organization, as discussed in the previous chapters, may have precluded such information requests.

All the groups, on the other hand, felt that the patient wanted a low-cost quality product. Hence, all the groups placed their assumption regarding the patient in the upper right quadrant.

We shall not bother to pursue here the further details of our methodology for resolving messy problems of this kind.[8] We shall merely note that the group of executives was finally able as a result of this process to agree as a whole on one of the alternatives to pursue. They decided to raise the price of the drug in certain key, test locations and to monitor very carefully the reactions of critical stakeholders, and in this way, to test the validity of selective, crucial assumptions. If one lowers the price of the drug when one could have raised it, one will never find this out from the response or behavior of the market. One will have precluded the opportunity of finding this out. On the other hand, if one raises it in certain test locations, one will find out very quickly if the market will tolerate this action or not.

Note that one can still continue to disagree with the company's final action from a variety of other perspectives, one of which at some point would certainly be ethical. Our point would nevertheless be that in either agreeing or disagreeing with the company one would still be making some fundamental assumptions. There is no way to avoid making assumptions of some kind. And therefore, they need to be displayed and examined in such a way that they can be debated. Far better to debate a question without necessarily settling it than to settle a question without debating it.

REVIEW OF THE PROCESS

Let us review very briefly some of the key features of the process we have been examining. We started out by explaining that assumptions are rooted in the behavior of some*one* or some *party;* assumptions, in short, pertain to stakeholders; they do not exist in a vacuum. The generation of stakeholders is a concrete way of getting at assumptions. Most persons can not generate assumptions directly. They are too vague, too hazy, too hidden from view. Asking people, on the other hand, to list the members of the set of actors, parties, etc., that are affected by one's actions is both a concrete and an easily accomplished task. We have never encountered an organization that couldn't do it if its culture was conducive to it. Once stakeholders are identified, it is then a relatively easy step to ask, "What do I have to assume is 'true' of a particular stakeholder (i.e. its behavior) such that *starting from* this assumption I can *then derive* or support my policy or my actions?"

Note that there is no guarantee that all groups will generate the same set of stakeholders as happened in the drug company case. This is thus one of the first ways in which groups can differ from one another. If they do, then they are making different assumptions about who is influencing or who ought to influence (at the very least be considered) in their situation. Many a group differs over "the basic right of recognition." As the modern corporation has grown it has had to consider more and more stakeholders than it did previously, whether it likes this or not. The same is now true of all organizations, public and private.

The second way in which groups can differ is in the qualitative form of the assumption or property they impute to a particular stakeholder. The physician in the drug company case is illustrative here. One group assumed price-insensitivity; the other assumed just the opposite. Thus, the process helps to surface fundamental differences of this kind.

Third, groups can disagree over their importance and certainty rankings. Thus, for example, two groups could conceivably both agree that the physician was a relevant stakeholder. Conceivably they could both agree on the same qualitative assumption of price-insensitivity. However, one group could consider this to be very important and very *un*certain to their policy while another could consider it to be very *un*important and very certain. The third step of mapping assumptions helps groups to *see* this. We have deliberately emphasized the word "see" because we believe strongly that often it is the failure to be able to observe assumptions that drives groups around in an endless circle. We have also deliberately emphasized each step in the process because the method, if there really be just one, for working on complex problems *is above all a behavioral process* for allowing persons to *see* their differences: over stakeholders (who's involved, who should be considered, who has the right to be recognized), over assumptions (what the stakeholders are presumed to be like), and over mapping (what's important and what's felt to be known). It is our feeling that many of the difficulties between our fellow men are as much due to the methods we use to examine those differences as they are the result of those basic differences themselves. We seem to relish organizing ourselves into forms that are designed to prevent us from airing and resolving our differences in anything resembling a constructive fashion. We just have to break out of this vicious and destructive circle.[9]

CONCLUDING REMARKS

This chapter has attempted to introduce a new way of thinking about complex managerial and social systems. In effect, it has argued that social systems are structured, organized, and constituted in terms of stakeholders. It has also argued that we need new methods for uncovering *systematically* important system stakeholders and their associated properties (assumptions) upon which an organization's plans and actions depend. Again, we have deliberately emphasized the word "systematically." It is the key word. Many organizations pretend to do what we are advocating but we do not believe that they really do it. They certainly don't do the thorough and systematic job of monitoring stakeholders as we are advocating here.[10] Little wonder why their policies atrophy as the world pulls the rug out from under them.

Likewise, it is easy to identify four stances, really pathologies, toward planning that often develop in each of the four cells in Figure 6-2. The authors have literally encountered groups that felt all their assumptions fell into the unimportant, certain quadrant. This group was saying in effect, "We know it all (everything is certain) but it doesn't matter (it's all unimportant)." Now, either this group is right or they are playing a gigantic game of denial. The authors tend to believe it is denial (i.e., they are denying the actual uncertainties in their environment) or they are not risking any significantly new ideas or products that would inevitably get them into the uncertain cell.

2. Another attitude is to say that you don't know anything for certain (it's all uncertain) but that it's all unimportant! In other words, you know that you don't know but you also know that it doesn't matter! This can be another defensive position. Again, we are talking about if *every* assumption a group makes or the vast majority of their assumptions fall into the unimportant, uncertain camp.

3. Another position still is to say that one knows it all and that it's all important. In other words, the group is really saying that they're in total control. Now this can either be true or very arrogant. When anything falls into one quadrant exclusively, the authors tend to be very skeptical. We find this very hard to believe. So do other groups who are listening to this group's presentation of their assumption map.

Finally, there is the attitude that contends that everything is important but uncertain. These groups tend to feel overwhelmed by the world,
if not experience chaos.

All these extreme groups need to be helped. Whenever an orientation is so extreme, so one-sided, the danger is that it will fail precisely
where it has ignored the concerns that its counterbalancing opposites
raise. But this is why the authors also advocate the creation of opposing
perspectives on problems of critical, major, importance to an organization. *If major differences in group perspectives do not naturally exist within
the organization, as they did in the drug company, then they must be created
by design if need be to insure that important dimensions and policy options
of a problem will not be systematically overlooked.*

Too much rides on today's problems to pursue them from one and
only one perspective, no matter who the advocate for any one single position may be. The most critical thing we can do is to examine problems *systematically* from several different perspectives.

POSTSCRIPT

In the years since Mitroff and Emshoff first worked with the drug
company, we and our colleagues have had occasion to apply the method
described in this chapter to numerous organizations, both public and private.[11] We have yet to encounter an instance wherein an organization
did not profit significantly from the use of the technique as long as the
organization's culture was at least supportive of examining its problems
out in the open. This is not to say it is perfect, as the next chapter will
detail some of the difficulties in extending it to the kinds of corporate
tragedies we have been examining.

However many applications one performs subsequently, there is
probably always a certain fondness for one's first application. One can
probably never recapture fully the excitement of learning and of doing
something new for the first time.

In the years since Mitroff and Emshoff first worked on the drug case,
we have talked about it many times in making presentations to organizations of all kinds. It still remains one of the clearest and cleanest examples of the method.

In all those years we never mentioned the name of the drug company
once. While the case doesn't disclose anything really proprietary about
the company, and while we weren't prohibited by the organization from
mentioning its name, we didn't see any point to naming it.

Then the particular example of the unthinkable happened that
sparked this whole book. Tylenol.

The drug company is McNeil, makers of Tylenol. The parent holding company is Johnson and Johnson.

Now we wish we could contend that if McNeil had regularly used our method that they could have, if not avoided the poisoning of Tylenol (we ourselves doubt they could have avoided this or any other tragedy altogether), but that they would have been in a better position overall to have coped more effectively with the unthinkable. Whether McNeil could or could not have coped more effectively or have taken more seriously the process of thinking about such threats, we will of course never know. This may be beside the point. The point is given that the unthinkable has occurred and occurs with increasing frequency, what can other organizations now do to learn from the tragedies of others? What is the utter limit to which the technique described in this chapter can be pushed in helping any organization confront the unthinkable? How can they think about the unthinkable before it has occurred?

NOTES

1. William J. Abernathy, Kim B. Clark, and Alan M. Kantrow, *Industrial Renaissance, Producing a Competitive Future for America* (New York: Basic Books, 1983).

2. Russell L. Ackoff, *Redesigning the Future* (New York: John Wiley, 1974).

3. Richard O. Mason and Ian I. Mitroff, *Challenging Strategic Planning Assumptions* (New York: John Wiley, 1981).

4. Ibid.

5. Michael Porter, *Competitive Strategy, Techniques for Analyzing Industries and Competitors* (New York: The Free Press, 1980).

6. See Ackoff, *Redesigning the Future.*

7. Ibid.

8. See Mason and Mitroff, *Challenging Strategic Planning Assumptions.*

9. Ian I. Mitroff, Richard O. Mason, and Vincent P. Barabba, *The 1980 Census: Policy Making Amid Turbulence* (Lexington, Mass.: Lexington Press, 1983); Russell L. Ackoff, *Creating the Corporate Future, Plan or Be Planned For* (New York: John Wiley, 1981).

10. See also Ackoff, *Creating the Corporate Future,* for another approach and argument for the *systematic* monitoring of stakeholders.

11. See Mitroff, Mason, and Barabba, *The 1980 Census;* Ralph H. Kilmann, *Corporate Culturing: Getting America Out of Its Rut* (San Francisco: Jossey-Bass, 1984).

7

Coping II:
Advanced Coping

The excitement in [the airplane] business lies in the sweep of the uncertainties. Matters as basic as the cost of the product—the airplane—and its break-even point are obscure because so much else is uncertain or unclear. The fragility of the airline industry does, of course, create uncertainties about the size and the reliability of the market for a new airplane or a new variant of an existing airplane. Then, there is a wide range of unknowns, for which an arbitrarily fixed amount of money must be set aside in the development budget. Some of these are so-called known unknowns; others are thought of as unknown unknowns and are called "unk-unks." The assumption is that normal improvements in an airplane program or an engine program will create problems of a familiar kind that add to the costs; these are the known unknowns. The term "unk-unks" is used to cover less predictable contingencies; the assumption is that any new airplane or engine intended to advance the state of the art will harbor surprises in the form of problems that are wholly unforeseen, and perhaps even novel, and these must be taken account of in the budget. Sometimes, as in the case of the metal fatigue that ended de Havilland's Comet program, an unk-unk is not discovered until crashes have occurred. The more conservative and cautious companies, naturally, allot funds for unknowns more generous than others do. Companies that tempt fate by failing to plan seriously for the unknowns are likely to pay dearly for their audacity.

John Newhouse[1]

INTRODUCTION

In this chapter we want to show how all the ideas in this book finally come together. In a word, coping with unthinkable acts must be part of a total process of strategic thinking. It can not be separated from the proc-

95

so what is strategic thinking?

ess of thinking strategically about the totality of an organization or institution. The reason is that unthinkable, tragic acts do not exist by themselves in some separate corner of reality. They are part and parcel of the *totality* of the set of forces, considerations, problems, issues, trends, threats, and opportunities which affect the modern corporation. As such, the unthinkable must be considered as a fundamental part of the total stream of activities undertaken by the corporation and which influence it. As a result, *all* of the failures to cope adequately with unthinkable, tragic acts are in the first and last resort traceable to fundamental and serious flaws in the methods that an organization uses to think about itself and its problems.

It's time to return to each of the tragedies that we discussed in Chapter 1 and to see the challenges that each poses to our abilities to cope. The reader is in for some real surprises. Contrary to initial intuition, what one might have thought is the hardest to anticipate and to control turns out to be the easiest, and unfortunately, vice versa.

TAMPERING, THE EVIL FROM WITHOUT: THE CASE OF TYLENOL

In the last chapter we presented a general stakeholder map for the drug pricing problem that McNeil, the makers of Tylenol, faced. As the discussion in Chapter 2 made clear, that map does not exhaust all of the important stakeholders who influence the corporation. To the "more rational" stakeholders of McNeil's stakeholder map a whole host of "non-rational" stakeholders must also be added.

There is another and more powerful way to put this. In the applications over the intervening years that followed the initial case of McNeil, we began slowly to realize that "something more" was needed to capture the fuller set of stakeholders who influenced the modern corporation. It proved relatively easy for all organizations to capture the more rational, immediately obvious stakeholders in their environment. Indeed, we were able to formulate a rather straightforward set of procedures for helping managers list the more immediate and obvious stakeholders in their environment. For instance, every organization has a set of competitors or adversaries, as well as allies, suppliers, regulators, etc.[2] We have yet to encounter an organization that can not list these kinds of stakeholders with relative ease. But more than these alone affect the modern corporation. But how to get at "these more" remained a puzzling question.

Our first attempts to get at these "somethings more" came to us in the form of the tale of the snaildarter.[3] The snaildarter is the tiny, three-inch fish that held up the completion of a huge hydroelectric dam project in Tennessee for years and at a considerable cost. The designers of the dam, it turned out, had not seriously considered the snaildarters in any of their so-called "rational" plans and cost calculations. The environmentalists, on the other hand, did seriously consider the snaildarters. The environmentalists pointed out that if the dam were built on the site where it was planned, then it would render the snaildarters extinct. As a result of environmentalists' concerns and lobbying, completion of the dam was halted under the Endangered Species Act until years later when it could be proved that the snaildarters would not be rendered extinct by the project.

The lesson of the snaildarters is a very important one. First, it says that, both figuratively and literally, just beneath the surface of the most rational laid plans of mice and men swim forces of which they are unconscious, and perhaps of which they do not really wish to be conscious. Second, it also says that potentially there are always other stakeholders (in this case, environmentalists) who do wish to be aware of these neglected stakeholders and who will take it upon themselves as part of their self-proclaimed, social obligation to speak for these other stakeholders who can not speak for themselves. Thus, for another example, the Sierra Club takes it upon itself to speak for wilderness areas and creatures that can not speak for themselves. Mother Nature or some such concept may "speak directly" to the receptive ears of the natural scientist but presumably she does not speak equally to those such as real-estate developers and engineers who may choose not to hear her.

The lesson of the snaildarters is thus a very, very important one. On the surface snaildarters are insignificantly small. However their true social impact extends far beyond their physical size. To put it succinctly: their true impact varies inversely with their perceived probability of occurrence. That is, from a limited perspective they represent extremely low probability of occurring forces in the environment, but if they do occur, their effects or consequences are disastrous. An essential part of thinking strategically is therefore concerned with monitoring one's environment for potential snaildarters. Indeed, most organizations with whom we have worked have generally found the concept of the snaildarter so intuitively appealing that we have had little trouble in motivating them to take seriously the exercise of listing potential snaildarters.

The trouble is that the best of intentions and motivations are no longer enough. The difficulty is that very few individuals are able to think broadly about their business or corporation. If they are successful, they know their current business or businesses and hence their contemporary, most easily visible stakeholders in their immediate environment only too well. But we have found that very few managers or executives are good at thinking about even moderately nontraditional stakeholders.

For instance, every organization is influenced by a stakeholder of some kind from the financial community. Every organization can thus think of a bank or a financial institution with whom they currently do business. Very few organizations however can think of how novel financial institutions might potentially affect their business. Indeed, financial institutions are often themselves the last to be able to do this. For example, very few banks really took Sears seriously as a potential financial competitor before it was almost too late. Recalling our discussion in earlier chapters, we don't seem to produce in great abundance the kinds of minds in our society that can think as follows: "What property does Sears as an institution either currently or potentially possess such that if that property were properly harnessed it could give us the financial run of our life?"

The answer of course was that Sears already had in place a successfully operating and extensively well-organized computerized credit card network. To be sure, to convert that *credit* network into a broader *financial* network, legislation had to be changed, no trivial matter or easy feat. But the point is that the banks had assumed—and wrongly so—that the assumptions or societal agreements of one era would continue unchanged for another. Hence, once again, the reason why we have stressed the importance of continually raising to the surface, examining, challenging, and constantly monitoring one's assumptions.

Now if managers and executives can't think about something so relatively mild as novel or nontraditional financial institutions, then what hope do we have as a society that on their own without any external assistance or prodding they will be able to think about such really threatening and nontraditional stakeholders as psychopaths? It doesn't take a genius to conclude that the answer is, "Not much!" The point is that the vast, if not overwhelming, majority of managers and executives have neither been educated in the first place nor rewarded in the second place by their organizations to think creatively about nontraditional stakeholders and the affects of them on their corporations.

The first step then in coping with whatever brand of the unthinkable is to recognize that *every organization has a counterpart organization, a hidden-from-view or shadow organization.*

The known set of stakeholders that an organization ordinarily does business with in its current, everyday working environment constitutes only an exceedingly small proportion of the vast proportion of stakeholders it must consider if it is to protect itself and to prosper. Most organizations have only an extremely limited view of the stakeholders who surround them. The *shadow* of an organization thus consists of all those stakeholders in the broader environment that the organization has either ignored or is unconscious of.

The term "shadow" is anything but arbitrary. In Jungian psychology it represents all those aspects of a person's personality that the person has either ignored or suppressed. The shadow thus represents all the ignored and/or undeveloped aspects of the person *which nonetheless must be attended to by the person's psyche.* The shadow aspects affect the person's consciousness through the unconsciousness as we argued in the chapter on the psychopath.

The shadow is also important on the societal level. It can be argued that the evil which organizations experience is partly of their own making. Evil is the result of all those forces acting on the organization that the organization has chosen not to acknowledge. The most interesting social theories of evil fundamentally have to do with the shadow of society.[4]

To borrow a metaphor, if you look at the stakeholder maps that most organizations with whom we have worked construct of themselves, they resemble tiny islands surrounded by a large sea of potent and largely unknown forces of which these organizations are for the most part not even aware. In other words, *they don't even know what it is they don't even know about.* The irony is that the self-conception of these very same organizations is that of strong and largely explored, i.e., known, continents. They think they are operating more in the known or certain areas of their assumption plots whereas we think they are operating more in the unknown quadrants.

This question of not knowing what it is that you don't even know is absolutely critical. Stanley Davis, a leading academic who is at the forefront of both business policy and organization culture and who has had considerable experience with a variety of real-world organizations, puts it as follows:

> I once asked an executive vice-president who was responsible for the future development of a very large corporation, "What is the thing you worry about most on your job?" His answer was startling. "I worry most about what my people don't know that they don't know. What they know that they don't know, they are able to work on and find the answers to. But they can't do that if they don't know that they don't know." The shift from (1) [not knowing that you don't know] to (2) [knowing that you don't know] is generally referred to as "a major breakthrough." This shift raises more questions than it answers. *That is its purpose. Before this shift, no one ever thought of asking such questions.*[5]

Davis's points can be easily illustrated in terms of the assumption plot of the last chapter. Figure 7–1 shows how the certain-uncertain dimension may be interpreted. Whenever we plot a particular stakeholder assumption in the certain quadrants (I or II), in effect we are saying that

FIGURE 7-1

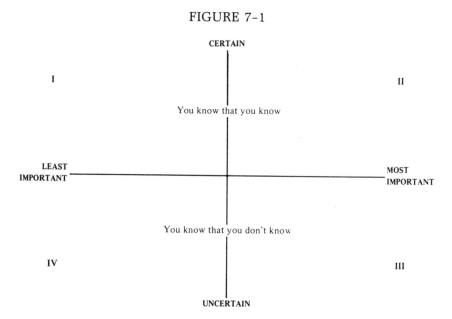

Knowing That You Know Versus Knowing That You Don't Know

we know what a particular stakeholder is like: *we know that we know* (i.e., we have certainty) about a particular stakeholder. Conversely, whenever we plot a stakeholder assumption in the uncertain quadrants (III or IV), we are saying that *we know that we don't know* what a particular stakeholder is like. The point is that everything that makes it *on to* a stakeholder map of assumptions represents what we know (whether it is known ignorance or known knowledge) and what we feel is important to know. All those things that do not even make it on to the map represent either (1) what we don't know what it is that we know or don't know or (2) what we feel is not worth knowing.

The first step in coping with the unthinkable thus consists of expanding our thinking as much as is humanly possible of the kinds of stakeholder forces that can influence the organization. The second step in coping with the particular kind of unthinkable represented by the Tylenol tragedy is to realize that potentially the most potent evil stakeholder who emanates from the shadow of the organization is that of the psychopathic personality. Notice carefully that we did not say that only psychopaths are capable of engaging in such evil. We say only that psychopathic personalities are the most extreme representatives of that portion of the shadow which applies in this case.

WE KNOW MORE THAN WE THINK WE DO!

The third step is to realize that we know more than we might think we do about the detailed stakeholder map that applies to cases of the Tylenol variety. Figure 7-2 represents a very limited and greatly simplified stakeholder map of just four out of the many stakeholders who potentially apply. While only four, everyone would recognize that they are four of the most important stakeholders.

Recall once again that it is not the stakeholders themselves who are being plotted but the assumptions with regard to what they are like that are being plotted. Thus, Psychopath K refers to the assumption that a psychopathic personality has struck or will strike against Tylenol. The K stands for known. Thus, the assumption is: It is a known fact that a psychopathic personality has struck or will strike against a major brand product. We have plotted this assumption at the highest level of certainty to indicate that it is indeed certain—it has indeed occurred—in other words, it is a fact. Indeed, a fact can be defined as an assumption whose occurrence or statement is certain.

While not every organization or group would necessarily agree with us, for purposes of provoking discussion we have also plotted this assumption at the highest level of importance. This is meant to indicate that every organization that deals in foodstuffs should take the Tylenol tragedy

FIGURE 7-2

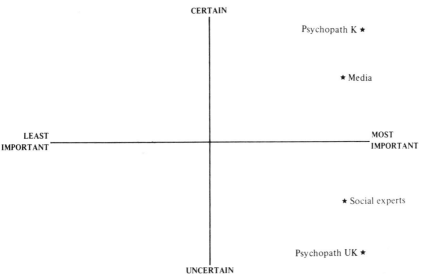

A Simplified Stakeholder Map for the Tylenol Case

extremely seriously. It serves as a societal warning to all those organizations who don't think seriously about their environment as to what can befall them.

Now any assumption that falls at the highest levels of both importance and certainty at the very same time is what we would call a "constraint." Almost by definition, if something is certain to occur and if it is perceived or judged to be highest in importance to the organization's behavior then it is a constraining force on the organization's actions. We are saying in no uncertain terms that the fact that a psychopathic personality has struck against one major organization should be viewed as a serious constraining force to be reckoned with by all other organizations.

In contrast, we have plotted Psychopath UK at the extreme end of uncertainty. The assumption is that there is an unknown psychopathic personality that will strike or is contemplating striking against a major corporation's products. For obvious reasons, we have plotted this assumption although highly uncertain as extremely important.

Now although others can certainly challenge our plotting of the assumptions with regard to Psychopaths K and UK, the difference between where we have plotted Psychopath K and Psychopath UK defines a critical gap in managerial knowledge. In fact, in our opinion it defines above all others *the critical gap* that management has to manage. The gap between Psychopath K and UK constitutes *the critical gap* that an organization has to manage. The critical question is: *How close* does the plotting of Psychopath UK have to approach Psychopath K *in certainty* before an organization feels it has to take action to safeguard its products?

There is unfortunately no general answer to this question. There may never be. It can only be raised for every organization to consider as part of its ongoing stream of activities in thinking strategically.

What every organization can do is to engage other stakeholders whom we have labeled under the general rubric Social Experts to help advise it in this area. For instance, in the chapter on psychopaths we argued that organizations need to engage those who are familiar with both the fields of business and of psychopathology to advise them with regard to the psychopathic vulnerability of their products. Most executives are neither prepared intellectually nor emotionally to consider such questions. Time and again we have found that executives are generally threatened intellectually and emotionally by such questions. They are first of all too depressing for the average person who has not had extensive training in social science to even consider. Second, they are intellectually frustrating since they are not the kinds of questions to which one can give a simple numerical, yes/no answer. This is precisely why we recommend that outsiders be called in to help organizations cope with such issues. While they are neither perfect nor infallible, professional social scientists have at least been trained to handle the anxiety which invariably accompanies such issues.

There is also a deeper reason for calling in outside advisors. By the very nature of such problems, the signals that emanate from society as to the increased likelihood of the occurrence of psychopathic acts will always be mixed. Very rarely will the signals be unequivocal. Only in a neat, mechanical universe is everything clear. But we don't live in this kind of world anymore.

Strangely enough, the signals will be mixed even after the occurrence of such acts. They are always open to reinterpretation. As a result, there is probably no single area than that of reading societal signals that is more critical to the modern corporation and yet at the same time is more problematic. But then this is precisely the reason why one calls in others: to aid in the exercise of informed judgment, i.e., judgment that is tested against the only thing we have to offer in this area, critical and even hostile questioning by parties representing the most extreme divergent points of view.

In the end, top management must itself bear the responsibility for managing the gap between K and UK. But it can no longer afford the kind of myopic thinking that kids itself that it can do the job entirely on its own.

Although they are not in great supply, minds which can help an organization take a broader view of its problems do exist. They have even recorded their thinking in forms such that it can be applied to problems of this kind. One of the best examples in this area must surely be the work of Russell L. Ackoff.[6] Ackoff's work is one of the best examples of expansive thinking that we know of.

Finally, in the case of Tylenol the role of the media was so powerful that it scarcely needs to be mentioned at all. Still, the assumption is that the media will play a powerful role in any future incidents of this kind.

It would be hard to fault J & J in its handling of the media in relation to the Tylenol tragedy. Indeed, some have contended that in the way J & J responded

> [It] clearly positioned itself as a champion of the consumer, gave meaning to the concept of corporate social responsibility, and demonstrated communication expertise that will be hard to equal for years to come. In fact, the handling of the crisis already serves as an excellent public relations case study of how to make the best of a terrible situation.[7]

While this might be true, the author from which the above quote was taken was also quick to note that it was easy for J & J to be forthright in this particular case. J & J was the victim, not the guilty party. As a result, it was able to generate enormous employee and customer sympathy. And indeed, J & J's C.E.O., James Burke, was able to harness to his advantage the fact that "the Tylenol contamination represented a new form of terrorism to which neither the company nor society could afford to succumb."[8] One would hope that if it had been a problem of their own making, e.g., through poor quality control, that J & J would have been as equally forthright. One would like to believe that as J & J officials tell it, "concern for the consumer is so deeply imbued in its corporate culture that it would have been unthinkable to act other than [they] did."[9]

The reasoning behind J & J's responses to the media reveals that in reality there are always a whole bundle of assumptions attached to any particular stakeholder. J & J's reasoning also shows how the assumptions that are made with regard to any single stakeholder affect and are affected by the assumptions that are made with regard to countless other stakeholders. For instance, listen to the words of James H. Dowling, president of Burson-Marsteller, the firm that since 1978 has handled the Tylenol advertising account:

> We felt the rebuilding of the brand would be accomplished *easier* and *quicker* if the *level of anxiety* that existed in the *general public* could be brought down to the reality of the situation. We felt the media was the best vehicle, the best conduit. *They* correctly created the alarm, but *they* also could participate in lowering the level of anxiety.[10]

Again, we see through Dowling's comments (assumptions) that a big part of the game is the management of anxiety. The executives of large corporations can not avoid thinking about the unthinkable because it raises anxiety in them. Although we sympathize with the desire to avoid anxiety, it's a question of facing and managing anxiety after a tragedy or that of facing and managing it before. Actually, it may be more to the point to admit and face candidly to the bitter truth that it's a case of managing anxiety *both before and after* a tragedy.

The fourth and final step we wish to introduce in this segment of coping with the unthinkable concerns the general issue of business strategy. Nowadays when business strategy still tends to get thought of primarily in narrow terms, e.g., improving one's financial performance as measured against the holy "bottom-line," we would do well to relearn that concepts of business strategy and of thinking strategically are in reality much broader in scope. Indeed, there is the real danger that because it is so easy to react negatively against narrow conceptions of business strategy and strategic thinking that they will be thrown out altogether with the bath water.[11] This is like concluding that because some people reason poorly, people and/or reasoning altogether ought to be banned. While such extreme actions (be it noted "strategies" for solving the faulty strategy problem) not only fail to solve the problem, they create worse problems as well. The cure for limited vision is not more limited vision. Rather the cure is to expand our vision, not to restrict it even further. The cure for blindness is not more blindness but an operation to restore our sight. Not to plan, to reject all planning, is itself a plan, and not a very logically consistent one at that. It can't even recommend itself.

Figure 7-3 shows the four generic concerns of business strategy that must be taken into account in analyzing any business problem. The four concerns or areas arise from the repeated analysis of issues across many different kinds of businesses. Experience shows that the general set of issues which the modern organization—public or private—must deal with breakdown into these four cells: I, Micro-Economic; II, Macro-Economic; III, Macro-Social; IV, Micro-Social.[12] These in turn derive from two primary dimensions.

The first dimension, technical/economic versus people/social, refers to the fact that in general, business issues tend to cluster toward different ends of a *content* pole. Technical/economic issues tend to be perceived

FIGURE 7-3

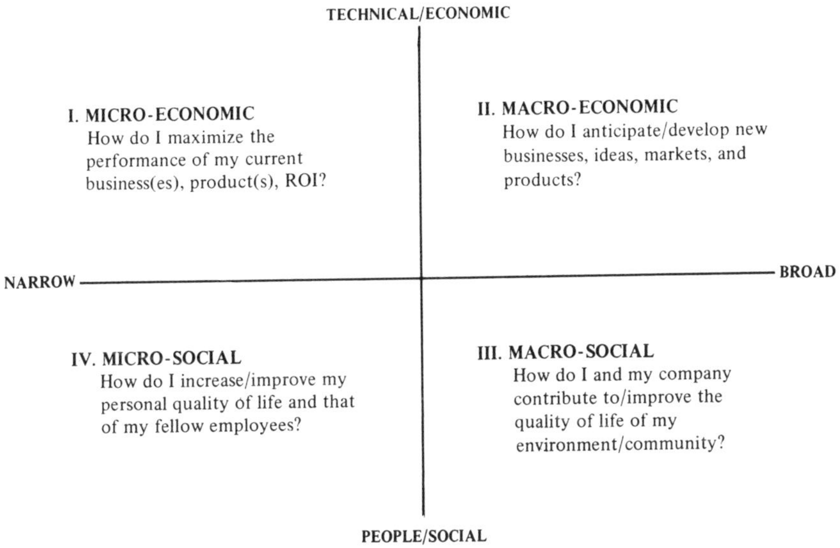

TECHNICAL/ECONOMIC

I. MICRO-ECONOMIC
How do I maximize the performance of my current business(es), product(s), ROI?

II. MACRO-ECONOMIC
How do I anticipate/develop new businesses, ideas, markets, and products?

NARROW ———————————————— **BROAD**

IV. MICRO-SOCIAL
How do I increase/improve my personal quality of life and that of my fellow employees?

III. MACRO-SOCIAL
How do I and my company contribute to/improve the quality of life of my environment/community?

PEOPLE/SOCIAL

The Four Generic Concerns of Business Strategy

as very different from people/social issues in content. Technical/economic issues deal, as their name implies, with matters of technology, production, manufacturing, distribution, quality control, information, finance, accounting, etc. People/social issues deal with matters of morale, motivation, trust, feeling, creativity, team play, ethics, corporate culture, etc.

The second dimension refers to the *scope* of an issue as differentiated from its content. Thus, issues conceived narrowly tend to relate almost exclusively to the inside of an organization while issues conceived broadly tend to relate to the outside of an organization or to its wider environment. Narrow issues also tend to relate to the immediate, here-and-now, i.e., to have a short time orientation while broader issues tend to have a longer time orientation. Narrow issues also tend to relate to current or conventional ways of doing things while broader issues tend to relate to new or novel ways of seeing or doing things.

Figure 7–3 shows the characteristic kinds of concerns that are associated with each cell. In each cell we have listed a single question that best typifies the dominant concern of that cell. *It is a testimony to the growing complexity of modern corporate life that it is not possible to initiate or to sustain any business strategy or policy that does not take explicitly into account the concerns of all four cells.*

For instance, there is no doubt that analyzed solely with regard to the kind of strategy it represents and not with regard to its merit, J & J's strategy to institute protective packaging to attempt to insulate Tylenol capsules from future attack is an example of micro-economic, or in this case, a micro-technical strategy. First of all, it obviously represents a technological solution to a complex problem. Protective packaging does not attempt to change people or to reeducate them. It merely attempts to prevent those with destructive impulses from playing out their impulses on a product. For another, it does not attempt to make use of new technologies even in the formulation of a purely technological solution to the problem. Thus, in every which way it represents the search for a narrow, technologically-based solution. This does not necessarily make this strategy wrong. It only types it as to the kind of solution it is and hence sets it off from other, potentially different, kinds of solutions.

But notice that even protective packaging can not stand on its own. By appealing to the media to take its side, to accept the idea of protective packaging, and to disseminate the idea, J & J was obviously dipping in to the Macro-Social cell. Further, J & J had to make assumptions that the general public wanted the product back (according to surveys,[13] they did), they would trust it (they would), and that the elderly would be able to open the new seals.

Cell IV, the Micro-Social, was certainly involved in J & J's overall decision to reintroduce Tylenol in that J & J soon realized that it not only had a serious *external* public relations problem to overcome, but that it also had a serious *internal* public relations problem as well. The depressed morale of its own internal staff had to be regained along with that of the general public's.

Finally, cell II, the Macro-Economic, came into play in that while Tylenol has come back up to a 32 percent share of the market, still the largest share of the $1.3 billion over-the-counter pain reliever market, it has not come back to the 37 percent share of the market it commanded before the tragedy. Still, 32 percent represents an outstanding recovery given the fact that its share plummeted to 7 percent at the height of the tragedy.

More significant still however is the fact that the Tylenol tragedy encouraged "competitors who had previously failed to top Tylenol sales to give the market their best [sales] shot."[14] The result has been the stiffest competition J & J has faced to date.

Finally, and perhaps most important of all, Figure 7–3 suggests that there are a number of other strategies that either in conjunction with protective packaging or acting by themselves could have been considered. Some of these may sound totally impractical or nutty at this point in time but the point with brainstorming impractical ideas is what feasible alternatives they ultimately suggest. Thus for instance, from cell III, could community self-watch groups be organized to monitor sensitive products in stores? Could this be done in such a way as not to interfere with civil rights or the normal conduct of business but actually to aid them? What would the positive and the negative side-effects of such efforts be? Could nationwide telephone community networks or hot lines be designed and implemented to encourage those with psychopathic impulses to call in and seek help before they act on their impulses? Should J & J help fund demonstration projects in this area? Why, why not?

And last of all, do all the manufacturers of foodstuffs owe J & J an incredible debt, financial and otherwise, for providing them with a "clear" early-warning signal regarding the potential threat to their products? In a world that is increasingly tied together, do we need to think about new schemes for sharing, if not spreading, the burden of financial disaster among the members of an industry?

In summary, there are three critical tasks the manager has to manage with regard to the kind of unthinkable under discussion: (1) the expansiveness problem, how much to expand the consideration of stakeholders who potentially bear on the problem, how many and different kinds of potential solutions to consider; (2) the uncertainty gap, how close to certainty an undesired stakeholder influence can get before action is warranted; and (3) the mixed-signal problem, i.e., the fact that the signals that society sends out with regard to (1) and (2) will always be mixed.

Note that the latter issue is not merely one of extracting a signal, any signal at all, from noise but fundamentally that of extracting two or more divergent and contradictory signals from the general background noise of society.

UNPLANNED, UNWANTED DEFECTS, THE EVIL
FROM WITHIN: THE CASE OF RELY TAMPONS

If ever there was a single category of the unthinkable that seems to thwart our best intended efforts to do something about it before it has occurred, then surely this is that category. If our discussion here helps at all, then maybe all it can do is to pinpoint more precisely what it is that we don't know in such cases. Actually, even here there is more that we can say than one might at first imagine.

All knowledge begins with categorization. It is the most basic way of giving order to the world. It is the most basic because it *names* the phenomenon to be studied in the first place and makes refined distinctions between different subtypes or kinds of the phenomenon in the second place. If you can't even name what it is you want to know, then one's worst fears have indeed been realized: *One can't even name what it is that one doesn't know.* All knowledge thus starts with naming.

If we can thus categorize a phenomenon, we have taken the first step toward controlling it. Imagine then our pleasant surprise in the course of writing this book to find an article in the prestigious journal *Science* that was exactly on the subject of categorizing technological hazards.[15] We were even more delighted to find that as the result of their analysis, the authors were able to pinpoint explicitly within their system of categories the kind of hazard represented by the Toxic Shock Syndrome.

The categories represent such factors as: (1) *intentionality* or the degree to which a "technology is intended to harm" living organisms, from simple nonhuman organisms up to human beings; (2) *spatial extent* or "the maximum distance over which [an event] has a significant impact"; (3) *concentration* or a measure "of released energy relative to [the] natural background"; (4) *persistence* or a measure of "the time over which a release remains a significant threat to humans;" (5) *recurrence* or a measure of "the mean time interval between releases;" (6) *population at risk* or a measure of the "number of people in the United States potentially exposed to the hazard"; (7) *delay* or a measure of "the delay time between exposure to the hazard release and the occurrence of consequences"; (8) *human mortality (annual)* or a measure of the "average annual deaths in the United States due to the hazard"; (9) *human mortality (maximum)* or a measure of "the maximum credible number of deaths in a single event"; (10) *transgenerational* or a measure of "the number of future generations at risk from the hazard"; (11) *nonhuman mortality (potential)* or a measure of "the maximum potential nonhuman mortality"; and (12) *nonhuman mortality (experienced)* or a measure of the "nonhuman mortality that has actually been experienced."[16]

A number of important findings emerge from the authors' categories. First, when given 93 important hazards to rate, the ratings of scientists and lay persons agree rather well overall although there are some categories in which there are tremendous differences between the two. This indicates that the categories are not only meaningful to lay persons and scientists alike but that they can be used by both to rate the potential of various kinds of hazards. Second, the categories capture better the overall range of complexities involved in assessing and trading-off technological hazards than the single and most commonly used category, mortality. Third, in rating 93 important technological hazards, the 12 categories clearly differentiate between the 93 hazards according to how they cluster on the 12 categories. The categories clearly show that there are some commonly perceived similar types or blocks of hazards. Fourth, and most important of all, the categories suggest a systematic basis for comparing various technologies with regard to their potential for hazardous threat. Thus, while we can not know with perfect certainty beforehand whether a certain technology or product will manifest a certain kind of hazard, we can use the categories to scrutinize all technologies and products for potential hazards in those areas.

In short, the classification of types of hazards with regard to their perceived seriousness provides a directed lens. It provides a systematic set of critical questions that must be directed to any product. Most importantly of all, it provides a set of critical factors that warrant the most critical monitoring from the environment. It directs a corporation what to look for, to be sensitive to. This above all is what a good taxonomy should do. It should provide a set of categories in terms of which to be constantly on alert in regard to the environment.

Notice once again that as in the previous section one can not keep from expanding on the problem. Figure 7–3 from the previous section is extremely relevant once again. Contrary to popular thinking, the basic problem connected with the type of unthinkable represented by this section may not be fundamentally technical but organizational or people-related. Once we have a good taxonomy of the types of technical difficulties to look for, the problem is no longer solely or even predominantly technical but organizational. How do we motivate, inspire, and reward the members of an organization to look for that which most humans wish not even to acknowledge exists in the first place? As we indicated in the chapter on organizational culture, the problem with coping with the unthinkable may at its most fundamental basis be that of designing an effective organizational culture that is motivated to admit that such tragedies not only exist but where members are rewarded (certainly not punished) for working on them.

Even in this most difficult area, the intellectual apparatus exists for thinking about the unthinkable. The problem therefore is fundamentally one of an organization putting its culture and rewards where they ought to be. Unless an organization develops a culture that encourages members to think about the unthinkable, most members of most organizations will play it safe. They will avoid thinking about the unthinkable like the plague. This does not mean of course they will avoid the consequences of a plague hitting them, only avoid thinking about it until perhaps it is too late to do anything but plan for their demise.[17]

UNWANTED COMPATIBILITY, THE EVIL OF
THE PARASITE: THE CASE OF ATARI

A moment's thought should be enough to convince the reader that although different on the surface this brand of the unthinkable is nothing more than a much milder example of the unthinkable represented by the Tylenol case. True, it does not involve the widespread and direct threat to people's health. But it does involve product tampering. More importantly, it is similar to the Tylenol case in that both involve the actions of what may be termed psychopathic behavior.

No one denies that in the case of Tylenol we are dealing with an example of extreme psychopathic behavior. The degree of psychopathic behavior is not as extreme here but it is important to see that it is an example of psychopathic behavior nonetheless. The justification of the actions by those who would commit an act in this area fit only too well with our earlier description in Chapter 4 of some of the major defining characteristics of the psychopath.

It should not be interpreted that this category of the unthinkable is not important in its own right. Its importance is that of demonstrating clearly that the threat of psychopathic behavior to products exists along a marked continuum. If as in the last section the threat to people and to products from technological hazards can be arrayed along various categories or scales, then the same is no less true of the threats due to psychopaths. Psychopathic behavior is no more all of one kind than is any other kind of human behavior. Once again modern management must consider the range of threats it is potentially prone to.

PROJECTION, THE EVIL IN THE MIND'S EYE:
THE CASE OF PROCTER AND GAMBLE'S LOGO

The last two kinds of the unthinkable that we have treated in this book are the most surprising. On their surface, they appear to be the very last things that an organization could ever possibly guard against. This view is wrong. It could only have gained the widespread belief it commands because of the incredible narrowness with which we educate current managers. Contrary to popular belief, the last two categories of the unthinkable are the most treatable. They are the areas in which an organization can do the most to protect itself before a tragedy.

On the other hand, we make no bones about it; the category of the unthinkable represented in this section is the strangest and perhaps most bizarre of all those we have treated. But as we pointed out in Chapter 4, the more bizarre the behavior, the more potentially analyzable it is.

This category of the unthinkable involves one of the primary psychological mechanisms, projection. As will be recalled, projection occurs when we mistakenly transfer an unconscious, inner state of our mind that pertains to how we feel about ourselves onto an outer person or object. Love or hate at first sight are the most dramatic examples of this phenomenon. Countless others exist as well, for instance, overreacting to one's superior because he/she unconsciously reminds one of one's father/mother. The point is that it is not necessarily the external personal object that contains the desired/undesired characteristics that are being attributed to it (although it can) but rather the person who is doing the projecting. For example, this often occurs when we react intensely, positively or negatively, to a person we've never met before for no apparent or good reason; i.e., we have no valid, outer objective reason to either like or dislike the person.

As the distinguished Jungian analyst Maria von Franz has put it, to truly understand the mechanism of projection "we would have to go. . .as far back as our animal ancestry. . .before we reached the point where [the] inner and outer [world] were *completely* undifferentiated. . .the [primitive] identity of subject [i.e., the person] and object [i.e., the outer world] still lives at the very bottom of our psyche, and it is only above that layer that relatively clearer, more distinct, discriminations between subject and object are, in many degrees, built up."[18] In sum:

"In the unconscious the inner world and the outer world are not differentiated."[19]

Thus, that projection occurs is not in dispute. Projection is one of the most firmly established mechanisms in psychiatry. Further, why it occurs is not in dispute here as well. What is at issue is how one can get a handle on dealing with it especially as it bears on the particular kind of unthinkable that is the topic of this section.

One of the most interesting things about projections is that they do not occur in random, disembodied forms. They are not disconnected lists of adjectives or properties. They hang together. They coalesce around rather clearly delineated clusters or shapes. These shapes are usually highly symbolic in nature. They are known as *archetypes*. Archetypes are the most powerful, extreme, symbolic images that the human mind is capable of producing and experiencing about itself and the outside world. It is not therefore surprising to find that archetypal images are scattered throughout all of the great religions, fairy tales, and myths of the world's cultures. Above all, these are the areas of human culture where symbols are especially to be found. What may be surprising is to learn that there is an extraordinary amount of agreement between the archetypal images of the most diverse religions, myths, and tales. As McCully has expressed it:

> Archetypes include such prototypical experiences as food gathering, elimination, fertility, father, mother, authority, self, femininity, goddess, eternity, childhood, circle, square, devil (evil), god (good), maleness, and sleep. If we look at the core or essence of a symbol . . . we will find evidence for archetypal influences.
>
> Since all men have created some form of religion no matter where they sprang up, religion should provide us with residues of concrete deposits of archetypal action. Christ and The Buddha symbolize some essence of archetypal deposit for us, since they are the religious representatives of our era.[20]

In his book *The Gamesman,* Michael Maccoby shows that archetypal images naturally and automatically appear in the context of organizational life. As such, they afford a unique, if not novel, way of understanding the influence of organizations on individuals and vice versa:

> One of Goodwin's [a "company man"] Rorschach [i.e., projective ink blot] responses expressed the contradiction and the lack of grounding for his goals. He saw fish, which he associated with the Christian faith, tied to a couple of court jesters teetering on the top of two docking spaceships. This symbolized his approach to corporate policy, an unstable combination of Christianity and the politics of the impotent courtier resting on technology in outer space. (The court fool tells the truth, but he is powerless.) He also expressed the contraction between the principles of religion

and power in the two historical figures he most admired: "Alexander the Great, he affected the future and was a great leader, but understood people and how to bring them together. And Jesus, he changed man without force, showed the power of working with people."[21]

One of the most dramatic examples of archetypes in action in organizational life concerns the recent findings of Paul Hirsch. In an article provocatively entitled, "Ambushes, Shootouts, and Knights of the Roundtable: The Language of Corporate Takeovers,"[22] Hirsch demonstrates that when one large business attempts to take over another, the language in which this is conducted is anything but subdued and impersonal. It reflects all the emotions, fears, and joys that one should expect to find when the spoils of winning and of losing are so big. *When one is in a situation that is so rife with potential uncertainty, exhilaration, conflict, and hard feelings, one should expect to see archetypal imagery being used to cope with the intensity of the emotions being expressed and to attempt to contain them.* Indeed, as Hirsch himself points out, this is indeed one of the fundamental purposes of the language that is used. It helps to insulate both parties, taker and takee, from the intensity of their *emotions.*

The takeover event in itself clearly conforms to a predictable set of scenarios or scripts. In the most neutral terms, this boils down to offer → decisions/actions taken → outcome [that is, if takeovers were expressed solely in the impersonal language of economics]. In the business world, this relatively simple diagram has taken on the far more colorful forms available from such well known popular genres as the western (ambush and shootout replace [the more bland terms] offer and actions taken), the love affair and/or marriage, warfare (replete with sieges, barracades, flak, and soldierly honor), mystery, and piracy on the high seas (with raiders and safe harbors). Generic formulations also entail the frequent appearance of mercenaries or hired guns (investment houses to whom most of the negotiating is delegated), and black and white knights (culled from tales of chivalry in which the distressed damsel is either undone or rescued). In virtually all formulations, the acquiring executive is macho and the target company [i.e., the organization that is being sought to be acquired] is accorded the female gender ("sleeping beauty" or a bride brought to the altar; reference to rape also is not uncommon).[23]

Thus, archetypal images not only exist in general, but even more important and interesting, they exert their influence in an arena where the uninitiated or the psychologically unsophisticated would least expect to find them, the "seemingly" all-too-practical world of business.

Unfortunately, it is beyond the scope of this book to present detailed schemes for either the recognition or the analysis of archetypal images.[24]

Suffice it to say that such schemes exist. For instance, two of the most systematic and extensive treatments of archetypal images are those of Nichols[25] and Neumann.[26] Nichols analyzes in painstaking detail the 22 major symbols which compose the deck of Tarot cards. She shows that they can be organized in a format which comes tantalizingly close to a "periodic table of the *human* elements or forms." The "elements" parallel and elaborate on the archetypes mentioned by McCully in the brief passage cited earlier.

Notice carefully that we are not asserting that we believe in the literal application of Tarot cards to business! We are asserting anything but this! Our assertion is merely that the Tarot cards need to be read (i.e., interpreted) in their proper light. They are a major repository of man's symbol-making capacity. As such, an analysis of the symbols inherent in the Tarot cards and the meanings contained in them helps us to see these symbols in contexts far removed from their sphere of origin. Indeed, one goes to such seemingly bizarre sources as Tarot cards not because we believe in them but because others have. Tarot cards are among the purest devices for gaining a window on the projective workings of the human psyche.

Another source we have found immensely helpful in bringing to light unintended and undesired symbolic interpretations of corporate logos is a twelfth-century classic. It may in fact be the single most important, self-contained source for ferreting out undesired projections. It is: *The Bestiary, A Book of Beasts, Being A Translation From A Latin Bestiary Of The Twelfth Century.*[27] *The Bestiary* is a book that describes beasts of all kinds, common, everyday, and mythic. Many, if not nearly all, of the descriptions are infused by religious imagery and symbols. Since the groups most likely to see unintended projections in corporate logos are religious, the relevancy of *The Bestiary* to guarding against this kind of the unthinkable should be clear.

To illustrate this more concretely, let us give two short examples. One is an example of a case of positive projection, the Unicorn; the other is a case of negative projection, the Monkey.

> Our Lord Jesus Christ is also a Unicorn spiritually about whom it is said: "And he was beloved like the Son of the Unicorns." And in another psalm: "He hath raised up a horn of salvation for us in the house of his son David."
> The fact that it has just one horn on its head means what he himself said: "I and the Father are One." Also, according to the Apostle: "The head of Christ is the Lord."[28]

> A monkey has no tail (*cauda*). The Devil resembles these beasts; for he has a head but no scripture (*caudex*).

Admitting that the whole of a monkey is disgraceful, yet their bottoms really are excessively disgraceful and horrible. In the same way, the Devil had a sound *foundation* when he was among the angels of heaven, but he was hypocritical and cunning inside himself, and so he lost his cauda-caudex as a sign that all of him would perish in the end. As the Apostle says: "Whom the Lord Jesus Christ will kill with the breath of his mouth."[29]

Now we are not implying that every symbolic use of either a unicorn or a monkey in a corporate logo of some sort necessarily involves these and only these particular interpretations (projections). We are saying that any organization would do well to have someone inspect and review periodically its symbols for their projective content, and especially, in reference to the symbolic atmosphere of the surrounding environment. Societies, like individuals, go through phases where they are more or less preoccupied with certain symbols than they are with others. These preoccupations reveal the current problems they are wrestling with. For instance, the current spate of hero movies can not be taken as a random phenomenon, e.g., Superman, Conan the Barbarian, Excalibur, etc. If only in part, they express the great vacuum of leadership and purpose we are feeling as a society. What better way to express this than in our longing for true heroes.

This section once again shows the need for expansive thinking in confronting difficult problems. We are truly aware of the bizarre nature of this material. No one is more aware than we as to how far the material of this section goes beyond that which is presented in a typical MBA program! No one is more aware than we of the bizarreness of our recommendation to call in a specialist in mythology to scrutinize one's corporate symbols!

Our response is: we didn't create the complexity, strangeness, and never-ending wonder of the human psyche. As professionals, we have been trained to use whatever tools are appropriate to do the job. Besides, different times call for different tools that are more appropriate to the problems of its times.

Despite the initial strangeness of the task, we have been able to get MBA students looking for evil projections in corporate logos without too much difficulty. If it's a strange task at first, it's also fun. They have no trouble whatsoever in locating such symbols galore.

Today's corporate logos are, as they have always been, a virtual gold mine for such projections. For instance, one is surprised to find the large number of products that somewhere in their design use a hexagram.

We are not saying that one needs to be absolutely paranoid about such things. One can't and shouldn't avoid such symbols of all kinds. It's an absolute impossibility to avoid all symbols for words themselves are among the most potent symbols that man has ever created. The basis of all language is metaphorical (i.e., symbolic) anyway. We are saying that a little bit of paranoia may no longer be a bad thing in today's world.

WHEN AN ENTIRE BELIEF SYSTEM COLLAPSES, THE EVIL OF BLINDNESS TO CHANGE: THE CASE OF "MONOLITHIC MOTORS"

At the start of this chapter we said that in the first and the last instance all cases of the unthinkable must be traceable to faulty assumptions. The case of Monolithic Motors is thus neither unique nor confined merely to this last category of the unthinkable. Indeed, this category is the most fundamental of all. It includes all the others as special, but highly important, cases nonetheless.

As we have stressed repeatedly, there is nothing more fundamental that an institution, public or private, can know about itself than the assumptions it is making about itself and the outside world. As a result, there is nothing more important that it can do than to periodically raise to the surface for explicit examination and challenge its key operating assumptions. This for us is *the essence* of strategic thinking, not fancy financial analysis, nor fancy cute BCG (Boston Consulting Group) animals (cash cows, stars, etc.). Financial analysis is itself only based on a subset of the entire set of assumptions that an organization must consider, thus it can not be the whole of strategic planning or thinking.

The previous chapter has described the outlines of a systematic, yet operational, process for raising key, critical assumptions to the surface and challenging them;[30] therefore, we need not describe that process in further detail here.

The particular problem of this section is not therefore that of how to raise assumptions to the surface nor of how to challenge them. Rather, the problem is how one can *maximally challenge all* of one's core assumptions once they have been raised to the surface.

Even in this area, there are some relevant guides. Perhaps the single most important one is an article entitled "That's Interesting," which appeared in an obscure academic journal, *Philosophy of the Social Sciences*.[31] The article is not only about what fundamentally makes social knowledge interesting but as such is itself interesting.

Murray Davis, the author of the article, makes the fundamental point that for something to count as interesting it has to challenge a sacred assumption that is held by an important social group. It not only has to challenge the sacred assumption but it has to present a strong case that there is a completely opposite assumption that makes more sense. Take for instance assumption five from the case of Monolithic Motors: energy will always be cheap and abundant. The reason this assumption appears so absolutely ludicrous today is that its opposite is so obviously much more plausible. The old assumption reads like an absolute fairy tale.

What makes Davis's article truly unique is that he has the insight to appreciate the absolutely critical differences between (1) knowledge that is not interesting, (2) that which is, and (3) that which is outrageous. If someone writes a report or an article that merely reaffirms the obvious, the likely response is, "That's obvious; so what?; who cares?" This is an example of uninteresting knowledge; i.e., it doesn't really challenge any assumptions. If, on the other hand, we raise to the surface every single one of your key assumptions and assert they are all wrong, then the likely response is, "That's absurd." This is an example of outrageous knowledge.

Interesting knowledge is in between. We have to challenge your assumptions enough to get your attention but not so much as to outrage you, i.e., turn your attention off. Unfortunately, the case of Monolithic Motors is a prime example of a situation that falls squarely into the category of outrageous knowledge. Every single one of the organization's key assumptions is simultaneously under severe attack and/or threatened by collapse.

This, more than anything else, explains why it is so difficult to think about this particular category of the unthinkable. The number of individuals who even for the sake of argument can challenge all their most sacred assumptions and the number of organizations that will reward such thinking are so rare that they are virtually nonexistent. No wonder we have such difficulties as a society in meeting such threats.

And yet, one of the most interesting things about Davis's article is that he shows that there is a definite method to the madness of reversing assumptions. Contrary to one's initial assumptions, there is a procedure for getting to outrageous knowledge, i.e., for countering all of the elements of one's belief system. In brief, Davis presents a scheme for inverted thinking. For instance, one example is inverting assumption number nine of Monolithic Motors: strict, centralized financial controls are the secret to *good* administration. The inversion is: strict, centralized financial controls are the secret to *bad* administration.

Monolithic Motors is just a thinly disguised cover for General Motors. There is no further need for us to persist in the cover. Table 7-1 shows a more systematic and comprehensive analysis of all ten assumptions that composed the belief system of GM (listed as M.M.'s belief system in Chapter 1). Table 7-1 shows the generic concerns or issues that each assumption represents. The table also shows a set of inverted assumptions that is counter to each of the original ten assumptions. The

TABLE 7-1

Assumptions and Counter-Assumptions for the Case of GM

Generic Type/Concern	Initial Assumptions	Counter-Assumptions
1. What business are we basically in? Who has basic control of the organization?	1. GM is in the business of making money, not cars. (The accounting and finance people have taken over control of the organization.)	1. GM is primarily in the business of making quality cars, not money. Any organization that forgets its fundamental purpose for going into business in the first place will not achieve one of its fundamental financial objectives. (The engineers and the accounting/finance people should share control.)
2. What must our posture toward innovation be?	2. Success comes not from technological leadership but from having the resources to quickly adopt innovations successfully introduced by others.	2. One can not give up technological leadership in a world that is more competitive than ever. One no longer has the luxury of time in a more complex environment.
3. How does the customer fundamentally view our product?	3. Cars are primarily status symbols. Styling is therefore more important than quality to buyers who are, after all, going to trade up every other year.	3. Quality plus styling are equally important in a more competitive market where even the cheapest car is expensive by past standards and where the competition is able to produce well-crafted and stylish products.
4. How much control do we actually have over our outside environment? How much can we	4. The American car market is isolated from the rest of the world. Foreign competitors will never gain more than 15 percent of the domestic market.	4. The American car market will never be as isolated from the rest of the world as it once was. Foreign competition is here to stay and it will always be

really insulate ourselves from it?

5. What are the basic resources this organization needs in order to do business and how available will they be in the future?

6. What are the skills and education of our personnel that we need to presume in order to do business?

7. How isolated are we from the shifting concerns of our customers?

8. What is our attitude toward the government? Who do we perceive to be our natural enemies, our allies, why?

9. Which type of controls are appropriate?

5. Energy will always be cheap and abundant.

6. Workers do not have an important impact on productivity or product quality.

7. The consumer movement does not represent the concerns of a significant portion [of] the American public.

8. The government is the enemy. It must be fought tooth and nail every inch of the way.

9. Strict, centralized financial controls are the secret to good administration.

significant

5. Energy will never again be cheap or abundant.

6. Even with automation, worker attitudes and skills at all levels are more important than ever.

7. Given the rising costs of all products, the increasing concern with the environment, there will continue to be some organizations that will represent these concerns. Any organization that ignores these concerns is dangerously deluding itself.

8. The government is a significant factor in the environment and as such it must be dealt with whether one likes it or not. It is too easy to blame others for those problems that are due to us.

9. Compulsive financial controls are the cause and effect of bad administration. There is all the difference in the world between a financial system that

TABLE 7-1 (cont.)

Assumptions and Counter-Assumptions for the Case of GM

Generic Type/Concern	Initial Assumptions	Counter-Assumptions
10. How closed off is our organization to new ideas from the outside? How open, how trusting are we? What's our organizational culture like?	10. Managers should be developed from the inside.	*controls* an organization and one that *enables* it to do what it wants to and should do. 10. The culture of an organization should be continually assessed to ensure that it has not become a closed system that is resistant to new ideas.

Source: Compiled by authors.

counter assumptions thus represent the strongest challenge to the original belief system.

It's not therefore the case that we lack neither the methods nor the tools for challenging our assumptions. The question is whether we have the will to apply the tools. That we have a fundamental need to change the way we do and conceive of business has never been more clear than before.

Some analysts have contended that one of the worst things that could have happened to GM happened recently. It announced a net income of more than $1 billion for the second quarter of this year. "[Its] earnings for the year will probably be the best since 1978."[32] What's bad about this? Not that it's making money once again and shows signs of turning around. Rather it's that new success is not only premature but it's still thought by too many within GM as due to returning to the tried and true, the proven ways of the past.

> The changes GM is attempting are greater in scale and scope than those of the 1970s—indeed greater than anything the company has undertaken since the days of Alfred P. Sloan, Jr. and perhaps unprecedented for any organization of GM's size and complexity. At the same time, many of GM's 45,500 managers have yet to get the message. One GM executive glumly mused last fall that from what he could see, no more than half the company's managers had really grasped the need to change old ways of operating. Overconfidence dies hard, particularly in an organization as conservative as GM. And of course it dies all the harder when sales and profits are moving up.[33]

What's sad is that what's true of GM is now truer of all organizations today more than ever before in our history. That the need for change is more drastic and more widespread in scope than ever before is clear to our best analysts of American business.

> Long runs of standardized products brought America unparalleled prosperity. True, that prosperity was interrupted by a great depression and by periodic recessions. But these were interruptions, nothing more. High volume, standardized production always restored prosperity.
> America has been unwilling to give up this vision. The present economic decline, after all, superficially resembles earlier ones. Many people cling to the hope that it is also temporary, caused by passing phenomena that have little to do with the underlying organization of American production—"instabilities" in Middle Eastern oil fields.... Once these scourges are behind us, so this reasoning goes, America's prosperity will be restored.[34]

If this is what the body of American business thinks, then maybe outrageous knowledge is not so outrageous after all. What's truly outrageous is living in the status quo—especially when the cracks in the assumptions upon which the status quo is built are becoming more apparent every day.

NOTES

1. John Newhouse, *The Sporty Game* (New York: Alfred A. Knopf, 1982). Copyright © 1982 by John Newhouse. Reprinted by permission of Alfred A. Knopf, Inc.

2. See Richard O. Mason and Ian I. Mitroff, *Challenging Strategic Planning Assumptions* (New York: John Wiley, 1981), for an extensive discussion of a fuller set of techniques for capturing stakeholders.

3. Ibid.

4. John A. Sanford, *Evil, The Shadow Side of Reality* (New York: Crossroad, 1982); William Irwin Thompson, *Evil and World Order* (New York: Harper, 1976; William Irwin Thompson, *The Time Falling Bodies Take to Light, Mythology, Sexuality, and the Origins of Culture* (New York: St. Martin's, 1981).

5. Stanley M. Davis, "Transforming Organizations: The Key to Strategy Is Contest," *Organizational Dynamics*, Winter 1982, pp. 64–65; underscoring ours.

6. See Russell L. Ackoff, *Creating the Corporate Future, Plan or Be Planned For* (New York: John Wiley, 1981).

7. Michell Leon, "Tylenol Fights Back," *Public Relations Journal*, March 1983, p. 10.

8. Ibid., p. 11.

9. Ibid.

10. Ibid., p. 13; underscoring ours.

11. See for instance, Walter Kiechel III, "Corporate Strategists Under Fire," *Fortune*, December 27, 1982, pp. 34–39.

12. See Mason and Mitroff, *Challenging Strategic Planning Assumptions;* see also William J. Abernathy, et al., *Industrial Renaissance, Producing a Competitive Future for America* (New York: Basic Books, 1983).

13. See Mireya Navarro, "Tylenol: A Former Best-Seller Painfully Makes It Back Atop the Market," Los Angeles *Herald Examiner*, August 28, 1983, p. 2.

14. Ibid.

15. C. Hohenemser, R. W. Kates, and P. Slovic, "The Nature of Technological Hazard," *Science* 220 (April 22, 1983):378–84.

16. Ibid., p. 379.

17. William H. Starbuck, Arent Greve, and Bo L. T. Hedberg, "Responding to Crisis," in *Studies on Crisis Management*, ed. C. F. Smart and W. T. Stanbury (Montreal: Institute for Research on Public Policy, Butterworth, 1978), pp. 111–37; William H. Starbuck, "Organizations as Action Generators," *American Sociological Review* 48 (1983):91–102.

18. Maria von Franz, *Projection and Re-Collection in Jungian Psychology*, (London: Open Court, 1980), p. 8.

19. Ibid., p. 19; underscoring in original.

20. R. McCully, *Rorschach Theory and Symbolism, A Jungian Approach to Clinical Material* (Baltimore: Williams and Watkins, 1971), p. 51.

21. Michael Maccoby, *The Gamesman* (New York: Bantam, 1976), p. 96.

22. Paul Hirsch, "The Language of Corporate Takeovers," in *Organizational Symbolism,*

ed. Louis R. Pondy, Peter Frost, Gareth Morgan, and Thomas C. Dandridge (Greenwich, Conn.: JAI Press, 1983), pp. 150–158.

23. Ibid., p. 236.

24. Ian I. Mitroff, *Stakeholders of the Organizational Mind, A New Approach to Organizational Policy-Making* (San Francisco: Jossey-Bass, 1983).

25. Salle Nichols, *Jung and Tarot, An Archetypal Journey* (New York: Samuel Weiser, 1980).

26. Erich Neumann, *The Origin and History of Consciousness* (Princeton, N.J.: Princeton University Press, 1954); Erich Neumann, *The Great Mother, An Analysis of the Archetype* (Princeton, N.J.: Princeton University Press, 1963).

27. T.H. White, ed., *The Bestiary* (New York: Perigee, 1980).

28. Ibid., p. 21.

29. Ibid., p. 35.

30. Mason and Mitroff, *Challenging Strategic Planning Assumptions.*

31. Murray Davis, "That's Interesting," *Philosophy of the Social Sciences,* Vol. 1, No. 4 (1971), pp. 309–44.

32. Charles G. Burck, "Will Success Spoil General Motors?" *Fortune,* August 22, 1983, p. 94.

33. Ibid., p. 100.

34. Robert B. Reich, *The Next American Frontier* (New York: Times Books, 1983).

8

Essential Lessons

The unconscious is not just evil by nature, it is also the source of the highest good.[1]

Carl G. Jung

Like so many complex problems, it is often easier to state a problem than it is to offer concrete solutions or effective strategies for coping with it. Hence, the reason why it has taken us an entire book to even begin to address such problems as corporate tragedies. As we have seen, the sources for the existence of unthinkable acts are many: (1) a world that is infinitely more complex as compared to that of earlier times; (2) an educational system that has not kept pace with the kinds of new concepts, methods, and tools needed to survive in an increasingly complex world; (3) cultures that are no longer sufficient to cope with the kinds of problems organizations now face and are bombarded with daily; and (4) inadequate theories of human behavior that are no longer adequate to make sense of the bewildering variety of forces that affect daily the products, services, beliefs, etc., of all organizations.

For all these reasons and more, this is why the "solutions" to such problems must be as equally complex, if not more so, than the original problems themselves. The sooner this fact is realized and appreciated, and no longer either fought or resisted, the sooner people will stop looking for quick-fix, Band-Aid approaches to problems that can no longer be contained by such simpleminded tactics.

The purpose then of this concluding chapter is not to repeat our entire argument but to stress very briefly a few key points. We have essentially four points to make:

(1) In every case, we know more about the unthinkable than at first blush we think we do, and conversely, we always have less knowledge than we'd like to have.

(2) Thinking effectively about the unthinkable demands some entirely new ways of thinking about and forming images of the world.

(3) The desire in both the individual and the organization to resist thinking about the unthinkable is so strong that this very resistance must be systematically organized against.

(4) Coping with or thinking about the unthinkable must be part and parcel of an ongoing, continuous process for thinking strategically about the whole of an organization; as such it is vital to appreciate the fundamental differences between what is and what is not strategic thinking.

KNOWING MORE THAN WE THINK AND LESS THAN WE'D LIKE

This issue refers to the two key problems which we referred to in the preceding chapter that the manager has to manage. The two problems are the expansiveness problem and the gap problem. In every instance of the unthinkable, it is not the case that the manager either knows nothing at all (has zero knowledge) or knows everything (has infinite knowledge).

The very process of expanding how we think about the unthinkable reveals both what we know and what we don't know about it. One of the fundamental purposes of expanding our thinking is that of revealing more broadly what we know and do not know about the problem. The purpose is also that of opening our thinking up to more and new options. As a result, thinking expansively is one of the necessary requirements in coping effectively with the unthinkable. It is not, however, sufficient by itself.

NEW TIMES REQUIRE SOME ENTIRELY NEW WAYS OF IMAGING THE WORLD

The unthinkable not only requires expansive thinking but it requires some entirely new ways of conceiving of the world. These new conceptions or images were discussed extensively in Chapter 2. In brief, the world is no longer a simple machine but a complex, highly interdependent system. As a result, simple quick-fix methods no longer apply. Indeed, the use of simpleminded gimmicks makes the treatment of complex problems worse, not better.

The preceding two chapters have discussed in detail the outlines of an operational method that is appropriate to this revised conception of the world. The utilization of this method not only requires a different set of intellectual skills but a different type of education and organizational cultures to encourage and to reward its use.

MEETING INDIVIDUAL AND ORGANIZATIONAL RESISTANCE

Individuals and organizations resist thinking about the unthinkable for a wide variety of reasons: (1) to protect themselves from unpleasant and painful events over which they have no control; (2) to preserve, protect, and insulate their egos from evil; (3) to cover/protect themselves from being blamed; (4) to put as large a distance between them and failure/evil as possible; etc. For these and other reasons, we can not expect the general body of either individuals or organizations to willingly acknowledge and to systematically attend to the unthinkable without explicit programmatic action. Without such explicit and systematic awareness and the desire for action, individuals and organizations will utilize a diverse array of mechanisms for resisting the problem: (1) they will deny the basic existence of the phenomenon; (2) they will grudgingly admit the existence of the phenomenon but will deny or downplay its importance to or affect on their organization; (3) they will deny that it's their problem; (4) they will contend that while such problems exist and are even important, there are no proven ways to think about them; and (5) since one can't have complete or perfect knowledge about such things, one can't do anything about them prior to their occurrence. Every one of these reasons or feelings are rationalizations designed to protect the individual and the organization from blame, pain, etc. As such, they are both understandable and natural much as soldiers in battle sometimes experience shell shock to insulate their minds from experiences that are too painful to acknowledge.

For these reasons, organizations must develop cultures that encourage and reward individuals to think about the unthinkable *within the context of thinking strategically about the entire set of issues the organization is or will be facing.* Individuals must be given the special education necessary to think about such issues. Such education is both of an intellectual and of an emotional nature.

Forming one or more groups to address the unthinkable may be required in addition to the types of culture change outlined in Chapter 5. The group is needed to help individuals from being overwhelmed by the anxiety that naturally accompanies the unthinkable. The anxiety must be shared, not allowed to overwhelm either the individual or the group. We

COOPERATION

have heard too many managers say something to the effect, "I can lock myself in a dark closet and allow the worst fantasies to come into my mind. So what?" Our response is, "Sure; anyone can allow himself to be overcome by anxiety and paralyzed into inaction." The point is that *paralysis is not the same as systematic analysis.*

The individuals in such groups need to be encouraged to express their worst doubts, fears, and anxieties but not to give in to them. As a result, outside facilitators who are expert at leading such groups are necessary to prevent a group from being overcome by their worst fears.

Ideally, participation in such groups ought to be rotated. Very few can tolerate prolonged contact with evil. Evil is contagious. The point is analogous to the training of psychiatrists. One of the reasons why it takes so long to train a psychiatrist is not just because of the strange and difficult concepts of the mind that must be mastered but because it takes time to train individuals to listen sympathetically to the painful material of others without having one's own mind being contaminated by that material. The stuff that comes out in psychiatric sessions is generally so powerful that the psychiatrist has to take care that he/she is not swept up into the illness of the patient. So it is with evil as well.

Ideally, participation in such groups ought to be regarded as an essential step in rising up the organization's career ladder. No one ought to serve at the top of an organization who has not been formally prepared to think about the best and the worst that can happen to the organization conceived of as a complex, whole system.

WHAT STRATEGIC THINKING IS
VERSUS WHAT IT IS NOT

We have organized in a table what strategic thinking is versus what it is not (Table 8-1). As we have emphasized, the unthinkable is part of what it means to think strategically about the whole of an organization. Notice carefully that it is not the case that the items listed under the column "What Thinking Strategically is NOT" are not important. The items in both columns are equally important to an organization. It merely means that they are different and that it is important to appreciate why they are different.

A FINAL NOTE
ON THE TYPES OF THE UNTHINKABLE

From the very beginning we have not claimed that the five types of unthinkable acts we have discussed in this book exhaust all the kinds that

TABLE 8-1

What Thinking Strategically Is NOT	*What Thinking Strategically Is*
Solving immediate problems no matter how critical they may be.	Anticipating future issues so that they can hopefully be seized as opportunities.
Solving current problems within the confines of current constraints.	Thinking about how future problems will render current solutions obsolete.
Concerned with current solutions.	Concerned with future assumptions.
Concerned with stockholders primarily or with a narrow set of current stakeholders.	Concerned with the broadest possible set of stakeholders and especially with future snaildarters.
Concerned with doing current things right.	Concerned with asking what are the right things to do.
Concerned with improving the performance of current businesses.	Concerned with asking what businesses we ought to be in and will be in.
Concerned with managing one's current financial portfolio.	Concerned with managing one's future issue portfolios.
Solely or primarily concerned with financial planning.	Concerned with the full set of issues with which the modern corporation must deal.
Concerned with short-term results that are measured solely on the bottom line.	Concerned with what the future will demand of the corporation in order for it to be successful on diverse measures that it will be held accountable for by the wider society.
Forecasting, predicting, or projecting the past into the future.	Thinking of as many diverse, radical, and even outrageous scenarios of the future as is possible.
Concerned with reinforcing the assumptions that have built a strong, successful corporate culture in the past.	Avoiding the failure of success by not converting past assumptions into a corporation religion.

Source: Compiled by authors.

there are and ever could be. Indeed, it would be unthinkable that one could know all there ever is to know about the unthinkable.

Our message instead has been that the unthinkable demands constant and external vigilance. This applies not only with regard to how to treat the recognized forms we have discussed but with regard to new forms that are constantly coming into being. Instead of having identified all the kinds of corporate tragedies that could possibly ever exist, our claim has been that the five we have discussed should be sufficient to get organizations thinking about the unthinkable.

It should also be noted that the five we have chosen to explore were not done so either lightly or at random. There is in fact a method to the five we chose. We tried to sample significant types out of an overall classification.

Figure 8-1 shows a classification of the types of the unthinkable we have treated. One of the major dimensions that is obviously relevant to any discussion of the unthinkable is that of intention. It obviously separates cases like Tylenol and Atari from Rely. One of the things that makes the Tylenol case so evil is that it carries the mark of intention; someone deliberately planted cyanide in the product.

Another dimension that is obviously also important is that of agency. It makes a big difference in people's perceptions whether the agent causing harm is due to a personal, human actor or an impersonal, physical/biological mechanism. This leads to our third and last dimension.

As soon as one introduces the first two dimensions, intention and agency, one has to, given the discussion of unconscious behavior in Chapter 4, introduce the dimension of awareness. The case of P & G's logo is a perfect example of unconscious behavior. By definition of the phenomenon, projection is not intentional but unconscious.

In reality there is of course a considerable degree of overlap between all the categories. There is an aspect of every one of the cases that falls into every one of the cells of Figure 8-1. Figure 8-1 thus only represents the simplest location of the types we have discussed. Probably the most difficult case to classify is that of GM's belief system. And in fact some who have read this book have questioned whether it is even an example of the unthinkable, a tragedy, or evil in the same ways that the other types clearly are. First, we would defend the proposition that it is an example of the unthinkable and in this sense, it is a corporate tragedy. What could be more unthinkable and tragic than the case where all of one's most cherished beliefs came crashing down at once? Still, granting that this is unthinkable, is this necessarily evil? Again, we would defend even this stronger assertion. Not to be aware of one's general belief system when it has so many consequences for so many people in today's world

FIGURE 8-1

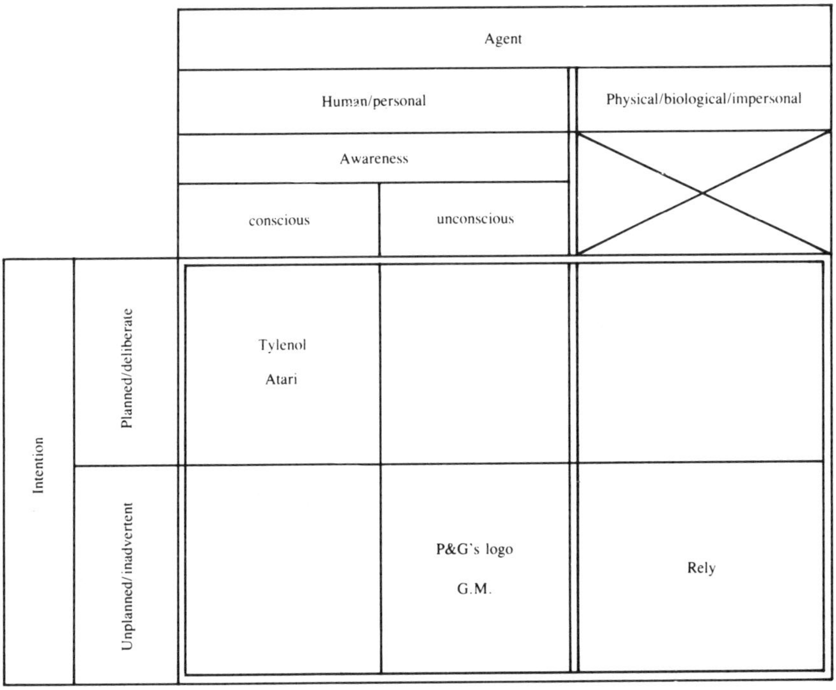

Agent			
Human/personal		Physical/biological/impersonal	
Awareness			
conscious	unconscious		

		conscious	unconscious	Physical/biological/impersonal	
Intention	Planned/deliberate	Tylenol Atari			
	Unplanned/inadvertent		P&G's logo G.M.	Rely	

The Types of the Unthinkable Treated

is to commit a kind of evil. At a minimum, it is a gross insensitivity to the wider environment in which today's businesses operate and influence. We would fail to do our duty as critics if we let business off the hook so easily.

More to the point of the debate, once one admits into the realm of discussion the phenomenon of the unconscious, the way is open for analyzing as evil any aspect of human existence that bears significantly on the conduct of human affairs. As the Second World War showed so poignantly, the concept of evil extends to entire national belief systems and not just to individual acts alone.

However, note very carefully we are not saying that GM's belief system is evil per se. The evil results from the lack of self-examination and the resistance to such self-examination when it affects so many people's lives.

FINAL COMMENTS

If there is a brief and effective way to summarize the entire message of this book, then it is found in the words of Yankelovich. Yankelovich hits exactly on the head the kind of intellectual traps organizations must learn to avoid if they are to be able to deal effectively with all the critical problems now facing them:

> The first step [in most so-called "rational" problem solving procedures] is to measure what can be easily measured. This is okay as far as it goes.
>
> The second step is to disregard that which can't be measured or give it an arbitrary quantitative value. This is artificial and misleading.
>
> The third step is to presume that what can't be measured easily really isn't very important. This is blindness.
>
> The fourth step is to say that what can't be easily measured really doesn't exist. This is suicide.[2]

If we have demonstrated anything at all in this book, we hope it is this: that we can not prevent all tragedies from occurring does not relieve us from the basic responsibility of thinking about them. If we have shown anything, it is that one can think about nearly every aspect of the unthinkable before it has occurred.

We come into the world naked with nothing save the ability to develop our minds with and through others. In the beginning and in the end, this is the only thing that stands between us and evil. Not to use this precious gift in the best way we can is the greatest evil we can commit. It is the greatest unthinkable of all. It is the greatest tragedy man can commit.

NOTES

1. Quoted in Emily M. Beck, ed., *Familiar Quotations by John Bartlett*, (Boston: Little, Brown, 1968), p. 936.
2. D. Yankelovich, quoted in Adam Smith, *Supermoney*, (New York: Random House, 1972), pp. 271-72.

Index

Abernathy, William J., 79
Ackoff, Russell, 19, 30, 83, 103
Activision, 7
Agent Orange, 32
Allen, Robert F., 63
"Ambushes, Shootouts, and Knights of the Roundtable: The Language of Corporate Takeovers," 113
American Multiple Industries, 6
Apple, 25
archetypes, 54, 112–14
asbestos, case of, 12, 26, 39
asbestosis, 26, 39
Asch, Solomon, 66
assumption analysis, 85–89; and collapse of belief system, 116–21; counter-, GM and, 117–21; map of, 88–90, 100–1; review of process, 89–91
Atari case, 6–7, 110, 130
awareness, dimension of, 130. *See also* psychopath

behavior, antisocial, 49–60
behavior, unconscious, 130; in-

fluences on, 50. *See also* psychopath
belief system, collapse of, 9–12; advanced coping, 116–22; M. M.'s core, 10–11
Bestiary, A Book of Beasts, Being A Translation From A Latin Bestiary Of The Twelfth Century, The, 114–15
Boston Consulting Group (BCG), 116
bounded-structured exercise, 41
brain, left vs. right side of, 42–46; and Rubik's cube, 41–42
Burke, James, 2, 104
Burson-Marsteller, 105
business schools, 35–38, 39; curricula of, 36–38; and human behavior, 49–61; network formation and, 37
business strategy, 104–8; four concerns of, 105
Business Week, 45

certainty, 40, 100, 101; change: need for, 121; planned and

About the Authors

Ian I. Mitroff is the Harold Quinton Distinguished Professor of Business Policy, Department of Management, University of Southern California. He received a B.S. in engineering physics, an M.S. in structural mechanics, and a Ph.D. in engineering science and philosophy of social science, all from the University of California, Berkeley. He has published over 140 papers, in professional and scientific journals, on management and strategic planning, organizational culture, psychology, and the philosophy of social science. His books include *The Subjective Side of Science, Challenging Strategic Planning Assumptions,* and *The 1980 Census: Policymaking Amid Turbulence.* He has consulted with such organizations as Diebold, Xerox, General Motors, Kodak, 3M Corporation, National Institute of Education, the U.S. Census Bureau, and the U.S. Forest Service. He is currently working with a major public television station on a business program concerned with many of the ideas in this book.

Ralph H. Kilmann is professor of business administration and director of the Program in Corporate Culture at the Graduate School of Business, University of Pittsburgh. He received both his B.S. and M.S. degrees in industrial administration from Carnegie-Mellon University in 1970, and his Ph.D. in management from the University of California at Los Angeles in 1972. Dr. Kilmann is a member of the American Psychological Association, the Academy of Management, and the Institute of Management Sciences. Since 1975, he has been president of Organizational Design Consultants, Inc., a Pittsburgh-based firm specializing in the five tracks to organizational success.

Dr. Kilmann has published more than 75 articles and books on analyzing and changing organizations. His most recent is: *Beyond the Quick Fix: Managing Five Tracks to Organizational Success.* He also has developed several diagnostic tools: The MAPS Design Technology, the Thomas-Kilmann Conflict Mode Instrument, and the Kilmann-Saxton Culture-Gap Survey. His latest research focuses on corporate culture as the invisible force that guides behavior.